Bread Machine Cookbook:

The Ultimate Homemade Baking Guide for Every Day. Cook with Your Bread Maker and Discover Perfect Easy Recipes and Tips for Delicious Loaves, Including Gluten Free Options

By Ivory Trivett

TABLE OF CONTENT

Introduction

The aroma of freshly baked bread is a universally cherished comfort, yet the journey to perfecting this culinary staple can often be fraught with complexity and frustration. The potential pitfalls are many – dough that refuses to rise, textures that miss the mark, and flavors that fail to delight. It's these common hurdles that can turn the art of bread-making into a daunting task. This book is crafted to navigate you through these challenges, providing a clear, accessible path to consistently excellent results, all through the convenience of your bread machine.

Your guide through this process is Ivory Trivett, who brings 15 years of dedicated bread-making experience to these pages. Ivory's journey is one of passion, patience, and persistence, qualities that resonate throughout this book. This isn't just a collection of recipes; it's a compilation of lessons learned, insights gained, and the joy found in each perfectly baked loaf. Ivory's expertise is not just in crafting delicious bread but in demystifying the process, making it accessible and enjoyable for all.

The bread machine, often underutilized or misunderstood, is at the heart of this book. Here, it's elevated from a mere kitchen gadget to an essential tool, capable of producing an array of breads that are as nutritious as they are delicious. From the essential basics to more adventurous creations, the recipes in this book are designed to offer consistency and satisfaction, turning the bread machine into your most reliable kitchen ally.

As you embark on this journey, this book serves not merely as a collection of bread recipes but as a practical guide to mastering your bread machine. Each recipe, tip, and insight are carefully curated to simplify the art of bread-making. This journey is about more than just baking; it's about unraveling the full potential of your bread machine to consistently produce delightful, satisfying breads. Welcome to a world where precision meets simplicity, transforming everyday baking into a rewarding, straightforward experience in your kitchen.

Chapter 1: Brief Overview of Bread Machines

Bread machines have significantly simplified bread-making, making it a seamless and enjoyable experience. This chapter unveils a comprehensive understanding of bread machines, covering their advantages and limitations, essential startup steps, and troubleshooting techniques, to empower you with the knowledge to master this versatile appliance.

Pros and Cons of Bread Machine

Pros:

- Convenience and Time-Saving: Bread machines are the epitome of set-it-and-forget-it convenience. With the ability to mix, knead, rise, and bake bread all in one device, they save time and reduce the manual labor typically associated with bread-making.
- Consistency: These machines are engineered to provide consistent results. Factors like temperature and timing are precisely controlled, ensuring that each loaf is as good as the last.
- Versatility: Most bread machines come with a variety of settings, allowing you to make different types of bread, from classic white to whole wheat, and even gluten-free options. The ability to control ingredients is particularly beneficial for those with dietary restrictions.
- Compact and Clean: Bread machines contain the entire bread-making process within a single appliance, minimizing kitchen mess and freeing up space.

Cons:

- Size and Shape Limitations: The size and shape of the bread are confined to the bread machine's pan, which may not always meet your needs or preferences.
- Texture Differences: Some purists argue that bread machines can't replicate the exact texture of hand-kneaded bread, often citing a denser crumb and thicker crust.
- Initial Cost and Learning Curve: While a bread machine is a one-time purchase that can offer long-term savings on store-bought bread, it can be a significant initial investment. Moreover, getting accustomed to the various settings and baking cycles to fully leverage its potential may require some time and patience.

Getting Started Guide

Understanding Your Machine: Each bread machine comes with its own set of functions and features. Familiarize yourself with the specific model you have.

Read the Manual: This may seem obvious, but understanding the specific capabilities and cycles of your machine is crucial.

Know the Capacity: Be aware of the size of the bread your machine can make – most range from 1 to 2.5 pounds.

Understand the Settings: From basic bread to dough cycles and specialized settings for different types of bread, knowing what your machine offers will enhance your baking experience.

Parts of a Bread Machine

Here's a brief guide to the essential components of a bread machine and how they work together to turn basic ingredients into delicious bread.

The Machine Body: The body of the bread machine is the outer shell that houses all the operational components. It's typically made from metal or sturdy plastic, designed to withstand the heat generated during the baking process.

The Bread Pan: The bread pan, or baking pan, is where the ingredients are placed. It's a removable part, usually coated with a non-stick material to ensure easy removal of the bread after baking. The size and shape of the bread pan determine the size and shape of the bread loaf.

The Kneading Paddle: Attached to the bottom of the bread pan is the kneading paddle, sometimes called a kneading blade. This paddle mixes the ingredients and kneads the dough. Most bread machines have a single paddle, but some models feature dual paddles for more efficient kneading.

The Control Panel: The control panel is the brain of the bread machine. It usually includes an LCD display, buttons, or a dial to select different settings and programs. Through the control panel, you can choose the type of bread, crust color, loaf size, and even delay the start time of the baking process.

The Heating Element: Located inside the machine, the heating element is responsible for maintaining the correct temperature during different stages of bread making – from kneading and rising to baking the bread. It ensures that your bread is baked evenly and has the perfect crust.

The Viewing Window: Although not present in all models, a viewing window is a handy feature that allows you to peek inside the machine without opening the lid and disrupting the baking process. It's a great way to monitor the progress of your bread.

The Lid: The lid covers the bread machine, keeping the heat inside and ensuring a stable baking environment. It usually has a hinge mechanism for easy opening and closing. Make sure the lid is properly closed before starting the machine.

Care and Maintenance

Cleaning After Each Use: After each use, remove the bread pan and kneading paddle from the machine. Clean them with warm, soapy water, but avoid using abrasive cleaners or pads that could scratch the surfaces. Ensure they are completely dry before reassembling. Use a damp cloth to wipe the inside of the bread machine, particularly the area where the bread pan sits. Crumbs and residue can accumulate here and may cause the machine to smell or smoke if not cleaned regularly.

Checking the Heating Elements: Periodically inspect the heating elements for food particles or residue. Ensure the machine is unplugged and completely cool before attempting to clean the elements. Gently wipe with a dry cloth to remove any debris.

Inspecting and Tightening Moving Parts: Over time, the kneading paddle might become loose. Periodically check and, if necessary, tighten it to ensure it's securely attached to its post.

Storing Properly: When not in use, store your bread machine in a cool, dry place. If you have a cover for your machine, use it to prevent dust from settling on and in the machine.

Avoiding Harsh Chemicals: Harsh chemicals can damage your bread machine's non-stick surfaces and other components. Stick to mild detergents and avoid bleach or other harsh cleaning agents.

Regular Check-ups: Like any other appliance, your bread machine may need a professional look-over, especially if you notice any changes in its performance. Refer to the manufacturer's guidelines for service and repair information.

Manual Consultation: Regularly consult your bread machine's manual. Manufacturers often provide specific instructions for care, maintenance, and troubleshooting.

Safety Measures

Placement: Place your bread machine on a stable, level surface away from water sources. Ensure it's not touching curtains or other flammable materials.

Electrical Safety: Plug your bread machine directly into a wall outlet. Avoid using extension cords or plug adapters, which can cause overheating or electrical malfunctions.

Supervision: Never leave your bread machine unattended while in use. Keep children and pets away from the machine, especially during the baking cycle when it's hot.

Hot Surfaces: The bread machine's exterior and the bread pan can get very hot. Use oven mitts or a cloth when handling these parts, and allow the machine to cool down before cleaning.

Regular Inspections: Check the power cord and plug regularly for signs of wear or damage. If you notice any, cease using the machine immediately and consult a professional for repair or replacement.

In Conclusion.

While bread machines streamline the bread-making process, they require a certain level of understanding and patience, especially when starting. Embrace the learning curve, experiment with different recipes, and adjust settings to suit your taste preferences. As you become more familiar with the process, you'll find that a bread machine is more than just a tool—it's a gateway to a world of culinary creativity and an invitation to explore the rich tapestry of bread-making.

As we transition from understanding the mechanics and nuances of bread machines, it's essential to build upon this foundation. The journey of bread-making, whether manual or machine-assisted, is steeped in tradition and innovation. It beckons a deeper understanding of ingredients, techniques, and the transformative power of combining simple elements under the right conditions to create something truly magical. Let's embark on this exploration, diving into the essential knowledge and skills that form the backbone of this timeless culinary craft.

Chapter 2: Essentials for Your Bread-Making Journey

Embarking on the bread-making journey is an adventure filled with the promise of warm, fragrant loaves emerging from your kitchen. This chapter is tailored for novices, breaking down the process into simple, digestible steps. Here, you'll gain insights into the essential ingredients, the magic of yeast, and practical tips for storing your bread. Additionally, you'll learn how to navigate common beginner challenges, setting you up for success in your new culinary venture.

Ingredients and Measuring

Measuring ingredients correctly is the cornerstone of successful bread-making, especially when using a bread machine. The precision of ingredient measurements can dramatically influence the texture, flavor, and rise of the bread. Unlike cooking, where there's room for improvisation, baking is a science that relies on exact ratios and chemical reactions. A slight deviation in the amount of a key ingredient like yeast, flour, or water can lead to a dense, dry, or overly sticky dough.

Types of Ingredients and Their Measurement Methods

Flour: Spoon & Level Method: The most accurate way to measure flour is by using the spoon and level method. Spoon the flour into your measuring cup until it's overfilled, then level it off with the back of a knife. This technique ensures you're not packing the flour into the cup, which can lead to using more flour than your recipe calls for.

Liquids: Transparent Measuring Cup: Always use a transparent measuring cup with a pouring spout for liquids. Place the cup on a flat surface and pour the liquid in. Ensure your eyes are level with the measurement marking to avoid over or under measuring.

Yeast and Leavening Agents: Digital Scale or Measuring Spoons: For small measurements like yeast, a digital scale is most accurate. If using measuring spoons, fill the spoon and level it off with a straight edge.

Fats: Dry Measuring Cups or Scales: Solid fats should be packed into dry measuring cups to ensure all air pockets are filled. Alternatively, using a kitchen scale can provide the most accurate measurement.

Sweeteners: Liquid sweeteners should be measured in a liquid measuring cup, whereas dry sweeteners can be measured in dry measuring cups. For sticky sweeteners like honey, coat the measuring tool with oil or water to help it slide out easily.

The Role of Temperature

Temperature plays a crucial role in the consistency of ingredients, especially liquids and fats. Ingredients like butter or milk should be at the temperature specified in the recipe. Using ingredients straight from the fridge versus at room temperature can significantly affect your bread's texture and rise.

Using a Kitchen Scale: The Gold Standard

While cup and spoon measurements are common, using a kitchen scale can significantly improve your baking precision. Measuring ingredients by weight rather than volume ensures accuracy and consistency, especially for critical ingredients like flour. Most professional bakers rely on scales, and it's a worthwhile investment for your bread machine baking ventures.

Practice Makes Perfect

Mastering the art of measuring ingredients takes practice. As you bake more, you'll start to get a feel for the correct textures and consistencies of different doughs. Don't be discouraged by mistakes – each loaf is a learning opportunity.

Essential Ingredients Simplified

Baking bread in a bread machine might seem like a complex alchemy, turning simple elements into golden, aromatic loaves. However, the secret lies in understanding your ingredients.

Flour: The Foundation

- Wheat Flour: The backbone of most bread recipes. It contains gluten, a protein that gives bread its structure and chewiness.
- All-Purpose Flour: Versatile and commonly used, but it may not produce the same chewiness as bread flour.
- Bread Flour: Higher in gluten, perfect for chewy, structured loaves.
- Whole Wheat Flour: Contains the entire grain and offers more nutrients but can make a denser loaf.

Water: The Hydrator

- Activator: Water activates yeast, starting the fermentation process.
- Hydrator: It hydrates the flour, allowing gluten to form.

Tip: The temperature of the water is crucial. Lukewarm (around 110°F or 45°C) is ideal for activating yeast.

Yeast: The Riser

- Active Dry Yeast: Needs to be dissolved in water before use.
- Instant Yeast: Can be mixed directly with dry ingredients and is ideal for bread machines.

Role: Yeast feeds on the sugars in flour, producing carbon dioxide, which makes the dough rise.

Salt: The Flavor Enhancer

- Flavor: Adds depth and balances the sweetness of the grains.
- Gluten Strengthener: Helps strengthen the gluten structure but should be used in moderation as it can inhibit yeast activity.

Fats: The Softeners

- Butter, Oils, and Shortening: Fats add flavor, tenderize the crumb, and help preserve the bread by slowing down staling.
- Variations: Different fats can add distinct flavors and textures. For example, olive oil can give a subtle, savory note.

Sugars: The Browning Agents

- Sweeteners: Sugar, honey, or molasses not only sweeten the loaf but also provide food for the yeast and contribute to browning the crust.
- Balance: The right amount will enhance the yeast's activity and the bread's color and crust, but too much can inhibit yeast.

Milk: The Enricher

- Texture and Flavor: Milk adds richness, softens the texture, and contributes to a golden crust.
- Alternatives: Non-dairy milks can also be used for different flavors and dietary needs.

Eggs: The Binders

- Structure and Richness: Eggs add color, richness, and structure. They help in leavening and contribute to a tender crumb.

Bread Storage Tips

Before you even start baking, it's essential to understand how to properly store your bread. The right storage methods ensure that once you've baked your delicious loaf, it remains fresh and flavorful for as long as possible.

Understanding Bread's Enemies

- Air: Exposure to air can dry out your bread, leading to staleness.
- Moisture: Too much moisture can create an environment conducive to mold.
- Temperature: Warm temperatures can accelerate mold growth, while refrigeration can cause bread to stale faster due to retrogradation of the starches.

Storing Bread at Room Temperature

- Cool and Dry Location: Store your bread in a bread box or a cupboard away from direct sunlight and heat.
- Paper Bags: Ideal for crusty loaves, paper allows the bread to breathe, maintaining the crust's crispiness.
- Plastic Bags: Suitable for soft-crust bread. While plastic retains moisture and keeps bread soft, it may also promote mold growth in humid conditions, so it's essential to consume the bread quickly.

Freezing for Longevity

- Slicing Before Freezing: Slice your bread before freezing so you can thaw only what you need.
- Airtight Packaging: Wrap your bread tightly in plastic wrap and then in foil to protect against freezer burn and flavor absorption from other foods.
- Thawing: Let the bread thaw at room temperature in its wrapping to slowly absorb the moisture condensed on the outside of the bread. For a fresh-baked feel, briefly heat thawed bread in the oven.

The Refrigerator: Not Recommended

- Stale Faster: Refrigeration can cause bread to stale up to six times faster than at room temperature due to the crystallization of starches in the bread.

Reviving Stale Bread

- Oven Refresh: Spritz your stale bread with a little water and heat it in a 350°F (175°C) oven for several minutes. This can re-crisp the crust and rejuvenate the interior.
- Microwave Method: For soft bread, wrap it in a damp paper towel and microwave for short intervals. Be cautious as this can make the bread chewy and the method is not suitable for crusty bread.

Preventing Mold

- Hygiene: Ensure your hands, utensils, and storage containers are clean before handling or storing bread.
- Check Regularly: In humid conditions, bread can mold quickly. Regular checks can prevent the unpleasant surprise of moldy bread.

Using Stale or Dry Bread

- Don't discard stale bread. It can be transformed into:
- Croutons: Cube the bread, toss it with olive oil and seasonings, and bake until crispy.
- Breadcrumbs: Pulse in a food processor and use for coating or in recipes.
- Bread Pudding or French Toast: Stale bread absorbs egg mixtures well, making it ideal for these dishes.

How to Overcoming Common Beginner Challenges

Venturing into the realm of bread machine baking can bring its share of trials, especially for those just starting out. This part is dedicated to helping beginners navigate through these challenges, ensuring a rewarding and enjoyable baking experience.

Bread Not Rising

Problem: Your loaf is more like a brick than a fluffy cloud.

Solutions:

- Check Your Yeast: Ensure the yeast is fresh and not expired. Store yeast in a cool, dry place, or in the refrigerator after opening.

- Water Temperature: Use lukewarm water (around 110°F or 45°C). Too hot, and you'll kill the yeast; too cold, and it won't activate.
- Measure Accurately: Too much flour or not enough water can lead to a dense loaf. Precision is key.

Bread Collapses or Overflows

Problem: Your bread rose too much, then collapsed, or it overflowed the pan.

Solutions:

- Check Measurements: Too much yeast, sugar, or liquid can lead to overproofing.
- Ambient Temperature: If your kitchen is very warm, the dough might rise too quickly. Try reducing the yeast slightly on hot days.
- Program Selection: Ensure you're using the right program for your recipe. Some machines have specific settings for different loaf sizes or flour types.

Crust Too Thick or Too Dark

Problem: The crust is more like armor than a pleasant, crunchy shell.

Solutions:

- Crust Setting: Use your machine's crust setting to adjust the darkness. If it's still too dark, try reducing the sugar in the recipe, as sugar can lead to over-browning.
- Pan Material: Dark pans can absorb more heat, leading to a darker crust. If possible, use a lighter-colored pan.

Bread Is Too Dense

Problem: The loaf is heavy and lacks the desired airy texture.

Solutions:

- Kneading: Insufficient kneading can prevent the gluten from developing properly. Check your machine's kneading cycle.
- Flour Type: Use bread flour for a lighter loaf. All-purpose flour can make the bread denser.
- Altitude Adjustment: If you're baking at a high altitude, you may need to adjust the amount of yeast and liquid.

Bread Has a Strange or Bad Taste

Problem: The taste is off, either too yeasty, too bland, or just not right.

Solutions:

- Ingredient Freshness: Ensure all your ingredients, especially fats and flour, are fresh and haven't gone rancid.
- Yeast Measurement: Too much yeast can lead to a strong, unpleasant taste.
- Water Quality: Chlorinated tap water can affect the taste of your bread. Try filtered or bottled water if you notice an off taste.

Uneven Crust or Shape

Problem: Your bread looks like it's trying to escape the pan, with an uneven shape or crust.

Solutions:

- Even Distribution: Ensure the ingredients are evenly distributed in the pan before the mixing begins.
- Pan Positioning: Make sure the bread pan is correctly seated in the machine.
- Dough Consistency: Check the dough during the initial kneading phase; it should form a smooth, round ball. If it's too dry or wet, adjust with flour or water.

Conversion tables

Flour

Volume	Weight
1 cup	125 grams
3/4 cup	94 grams
2/3 cup	83 grams
1/2 cup	62 grams
1/3 cup	42 grams
1/4 cup	31 grams
1 tablespoon	8 grams
1 teaspoon	3 grams

Powdered Sugar & Cocoa

Volume	Weight
1 cup	120 grams
3/4 cup	90 grams
2/3 cup	80 grams
1/2 cup	60 grams
1/3 cup	40 grams
1/4 cup	30 grams
1 tablespoon	7.5 grams
1 teaspoon	2.5 grams

Granulated Sugar

Volume	Weight
1 cup	200 grams
3/4 cup	150 grams
2/3 cup	133 grams
1/2 cup	100 grams
1/3 cup	67 grams
1/4 cup	50 grams
1 tablespoon	12.5 grams
1 teaspoon	4.2 grams

Liquids (Water, Milk, Heavy Cream)

Volume	Fluid	Mililtrs	Weight
1 cup	8 fl oz	240 ml	240 grams
3/4 cup	6 fl oz	180 ml	180 grams
2/3 cup	5.33 fl oz	160 ml	160 grams
1/2 cup	4 fl oz	120 ml	120 grams
1/3 cup	2.67 fl oz	80 ml	80 grams
1/4 cup	2 fl oz	60 ml	60 grams
1 tablespoon	1/2 fl oz	15 ml	15 grams
1 teaspoon	1/6 fl oz	5 ml	5 grams

Butter

Volume	Weight	Sticks	Ounces
1 cup	226.8 g	2 sticks	8 oz
3/4 cup	170.1 g	1 ½ stick	6 oz
2/3 cup	151.2 g	1 ⅓ sticks	5.33 oz
1/2 cup	113.4 g	1 stick	4 oz
1/3 cup	75.6 g	2/3 stick	2.67 oz
1/4 cup	56.7 g	1/2 stick	2 oz
1 tablespoon	14.2 g	1/8 stick	0.5 oz
1 teaspoon	4.7 g	1/24 stick	0.17 oz

Quick Yeast Conversion

Active Dry Yeast	Instant Yeast	Fresh Yeast
1 teaspoon	3/4 teaspoon	2 teaspoons
1 tablespoon	2 ¼ teaspoons	1 tablespoon
1 packet (2 ¼ teaspoons)	1 ¾ teaspoons	18 grams

As you turn the pages of previous chapters, you're now armed with the insights and solutions to navigate through the early stages of bread machine baking. With a clear understanding of the common hurdles and the knowledge on how to gracefully overcome them, you are well-prepared to embark on your baking journey. The recipes ahead are not just a collection of ingredients and instructions, but a canvas for your newfound skills and confidence. You are ready to proceed directly to the recipes, where each ingredient and step will come together under your careful guidance, transforming simple elements into exquisite, aromatic loaves of bread. Happy baking!

Chapter 3: Simple White Breads

A. Classic White Bread Recipes

1. *Basic White Bread*

Prep Time: 10 minutes | Cook Time: 3 hours

1 ½ Pounds Loaf (≈ 12 slices):

- 1 ½ cups lukewarm water
- 2 tablespoons olive oil
- 2 tablespoons sugar
- 1 ½ teaspoons salt
- 4 cups all-purpose flour
- 2 ¼ teaspoons (1 packet) bread machine yeast

2 Pounds Loaf (≈ 16 slices):

- 2 cups lukewarm water
- 2 ½ tablespoons olive oil
- 2 ½ tablespoons sugar
- 2 teaspoons salt
- 5 ⅓ cups all-purpose flour
- 3 teaspoons bread machine yeast

Directions:

1. Add the ingredients to the bread machine pan in the order recommended by the manufacturer, usually liquids first, then dry ingredients, and yeast last.
2. Set the bread machine to the basic or white bread setting with a medium crust.
3. Press start. The bread machine will mix, knead, rise, and bake the bread.
4. Once done, carefully remove the bread from the pan and let it cool on a wire rack before slicing.

Nutritional per Serving: 130 calories, 4g protein, 25g carbohydrates, 2g fat, 1g fiber, 0mg cholesterol, 290mg sodium, 50mg potassium.

Tip: For a softer crust, brush the top of the bread with butter or olive oil right after baking.

2. *Soft and Buttery White Bread*

Prep time: 10 minutes | Cook time: 3 hours

1 ½ Pounds Loaf (≈ 12 slices):

- 1 ¼ cups lukewarm water
- 2 tablespoons sugar
- 2 tablespoons unsalted butter, softened
- 1 teaspoon salt
- 3 ½ cups bread flour
- 2 teaspoons bread machine yeast

2 Pounds Loaf (≈ 16 slices):

- 1 ⅔ cups lukewarm water
- 2 ½ tablespoons sugar
- 2 ½ tablespoons unsalted butter, softened
- 1 ¼ teaspoons salt
- 4 ⅓ cups bread flour
- 2 ½ teaspoons bread machine yeast

Directions:

1. Place the ingredients in the bread machine pan in the order recommended by the manufacturer.
2. Select the Basic or White Bread setting, and choose a light or medium crust.
3. Start the bread machine. After the baking cycle ends, remove the bread from the pan and transfer it to a wire rack to cool.
4. Let the bread cool completely before slicing to ensure the perfect texture.

Nutritional per Serving: 180 calories, 6g protein, 34g carbohydrates, 2g fat, 1g fiber, 0mg cholesterol, 290mg sodium, 100mg potassium.

Tip: For an extra glossy and soft crust, brush the top of the loaf with melted butter immediately after baking.

3. Honey White Bread

Prep time: 10 minutes | Cook time: 3 hours

1 ½ Pounds Loaf (≈ 12 slices):

- 1 cup + 1 tablespoon lukewarm water
- 2 tablespoons honey
- 2 tablespoons unsalted butter, softened
- 1 ½ teaspoons salt
- 3 cups bread flour
- 1 ½ teaspoons bread machine yeast or active dry yeast

2 Pounds Loaf (≈ 16 slices):

- 1 ⅓ cups lukewarm water
- 3 tablespoons honey
- 3 tablespoons unsalted butter, softened
- 2 teaspoons salt
- 4 cups bread flour
- 2 teaspoons bread machine yeast or active dry yeast

Directions:

1. Add the water, honey, butter, and salt to the bread machine pan.
2. Next, add the flour, ensuring it covers the liquid. Make a small indentation in the center of the flour and add the yeast.
3. Select the Basic or White Bread setting on your bread machine. Choose the crust color if your machine has this feature.
4. After the baking cycle is finished, carefully remove the bread from the pan and allow it to cool on a wire rack before slicing.

Nutritional per Serving: 160 calories, 4g protein, 28g carbohydrates, 3g fat, 1g fiber, 7mg cholesterol, 300mg sodium, 60mg potassium.

Tip: Ensure your honey is at room temperature to blend smoothly with the other ingredients.

4. Classic White Bread with Milk

Prep time: 10 minutes | Cook time: 3 hours

1 ½ Pounds Loaf (≈ 12 slices):

- 1 cup + 2 tablespoons milk, lukewarm
- 2 tablespoons sugar
- 2 tablespoons unsalted butter, softened
- 1 ½ teaspoons salt
- 3 ¼ cups bread flour
- 1 ½ teaspoons bread machine yeast or active dry yeast

2 Pounds Loaf (≈ 16 slices):

- 1 ⅓ cups milk, lukewarm
- 2 ½ tablespoons sugar
- 3 tablespoons unsalted butter, softened
- 2 teaspoons salt
- 4 ⅓ cups bread flour
- 2 teaspoons bread machine yeast or active dry yeast

Directions:

1. Place milk, sugar, butter, and salt into the bread machine pan.
2. Add the flour, covering the liquid ingredients. Make a small well in the center of the flour and carefully add the yeast.
3. Select the Basic or White Bread setting on your bread machine. Choose the crust color if your machine has this option.
4. Once the baking cycle is complete, carefully remove the bread from the pan and let it cool on a wire rack before slicing.

Nutritional per Serving: 160 calories, 5g protein, 28g carbohydrates, 3g fat, 1g fiber, 10mg cholesterol, 300mg sodium, 80mg potassium.

Tip: For a richer taste and tender crumb, use whole milk at room temperature.

B. French Bread Recipes

5. *Classic French Bread*

Prep time: 15 minutes | Cook time: 3 hours 30 minutes

1 ½ Pounds Loaf (≈ 12 slices):

- 1 cup lukewarm water
- 1 ½ teaspoons salt
- 1 ½ teaspoons sugar
- 3 ½ cups bread flour
- 1 ½ teaspoons bread machine yeast or active dry yeast

2 Pounds Loaf (≈ 16 slices):

- 1 ⅓ cups lukewarm water
- 2 teaspoons salt
- 2 teaspoons sugar
- 4 ⅔ cups bread flour
- 2 teaspoons bread machine yeast or active dry yeast

Directions:

1. Pour water into the bread machine pan. Then add salt, sugar, and flour to the pan. Make a small well in the flour and add the yeast into it.
2. Set your bread machine to the French Bread cycle. Select the crust color if your machine has this feature.
3. Once the bread is done, remove it from the pan and let it cool on a wire rack for at least 20 minutes before slicing.

Nutritional per Serving: 160 calories, 5g protein, 32g carbohydrates, 1g fat, 2g fiber, 0mg cholesterol, 290mg sodium, 100mg potassium.

Tip: For a crispier crust, place a shallow pan of water on the lower rack of your oven during baking.

6. *Rustic French Bread*

Prep time: 15 minutes |Cook time: 3 hours 35 minutes

1 ½ Pounds Loaf (≈ 12 slices):

- 1 cup + 1 tablespoon lukewarm water
- 1 ½ teaspoons salt
- 1 tablespoon sugar
- 3 cups bread flour
- 1 ½ teaspoons bread machine yeast or active dry yeast

2 Pounds Loaf (≈ 16 slices):

- 1 ⅓ cups lukewarm water
- 2 teaspoons salt
- 1 ½ tablespoons sugar
- 4 cups bread flour
- 2 teaspoons bread machine yeast or active dry yeast

Directions:

1. Place the water, salt, sugar, and flour into the bread machine pan in the order recommended by the manufacturer.
2. Make a small well in the flour and add the yeast.
3. Select the French Bread cycle on your bread machine. Choose the crust color if your machine has this feature.
4. Once the cycle is complete, carefully remove the bread from the pan and let it cool on a wire rack before slicing.

Nutritional per Serving: 160 calories, 5g protein, 32g carbohydrates, 1g fat, 1g fiber, 0mg cholesterol, 290mg sodium, 70mg potassium.

Tip: For a more rustic crust, spray the loaf with water before baking and several times during the first 10 minutes of baking.

7. Sweet French Bread

Prep time: 15 minutes | Cook time: 3 hours 25 minutes

1 ½ Pounds Loaf (≈ 12 slices):

- 1 cup + 2 tablespoons lukewarm water
- 1 ½ tablespoons sugar
- 2 tablespoons unsalted butter, softened
- 1 ½ teaspoons salt
- 3 ⅓ cups bread flour
- 2 teaspoons bread machine yeast or active dry yeast

2 Pounds Loaf (≈ 16 slices):

- 1 ⅓ cups water lukewarm water
- 2 tablespoons sugar
- 3 tablespoons unsalted butter, softened
- 2 teaspoons salt
- 4 ¼ cups bread flour
- 2 ½ teaspoons bread machine yeast or active dry yeast

Directions:

1. Place the water, sugar, butter, and salt into the bread machine pan.
2. Add the flour on top of the liquid ingredients. Make a small indentation in the center of the flour and carefully pour the yeast into it.
3. Select the Sweet Bread cycle on your bread machine. Choose the crust color if your machine has this feature.
4. After the baking cycle is complete, carefully remove the bread from the pan and allow it to cool on a wire rack before slicing.

Nutritional per Serving: 180 calories, 4g protein, 34g carbohydrates, 2.5g fat, 1g fiber, 5mg cholesterol, 300mg sodium, 80mg potassium.

Tip: For an extra glossy and sweet crust, brush the top of the loaf with honey mixed with a little water as soon as it comes out of the bread machine.

8. French Baguette

Prep time: 15 minutes | Cook time: 3 hours 40 minutes

1 ½ Pounds Loaf (≈ 12 slices):

- 1 cup + 2 tablespoons lukewarm water
- 1 ½ teaspoons salt
- 3 ½ cups bread flour
- 2 teaspoons sugar
- 1 ½ teaspoons bread machine yeast or active dry yeast

2 Pounds Loaf (≈ 16 slices):

- 1 ⅓ cups lukewarm water
- 2 teaspoons salt
- 4 ⅔ cups bread flour
- 2 ½ teaspoons sugar
- 2 teaspoons bread machine yeast or active dry yeast

Directions:

1. Add water, salt, sugar, and flour to the bread machine pan in the order recommended by the manufacturer. Make a small indentation in the flour and add the yeast.
2. Set your bread machine to the Dough cycle. When the cycle is complete, remove the dough and shape it into a long, thin loaf or divide it to make smaller baguettes.
3. Place the shaped dough onto a baking sheet, cover it with a clean kitchen towel, and let it rise in a warm place for about 30 minutes.
4. Preheat your oven to 425°F(220°). Make shallow diagonal slashes on top of the risen dough. Bake in the preheated oven for about 25 minutes or until golden brown.

Nutritional per Serving: 140 calories, 4g protein, 29g carbohydrates, 0.5g fat, 1g fiber, 0mg cholesterol, 290mg sodium, 60mg potassium.

Tip: Mist the oven with water before placing the dough inside to create a crispier crust.

C. Sandwich Bread Recipes

9. *Easy White Sandwich Bread*

Prep time: 10 minutes | Cook time: 3 hours

1 ½ Pounds Loaf (≈ 12 slices):

- 1 cup + 1 tablespoon lukewarm water
- 2 tablespoons unsalted butter, softened
- 1 ½ teaspoons salt
- 3 cups bread flour
- 2 tablespoons sugar
- 1 ½ teaspoons bread machine yeast or active dry yeast

2 Pounds Loaf (≈ 16 slices):

- 1 ⅓ cups water
- 3 tablespoons unsalted butter, softened
- 2 teaspoons salt
- 4 cups bread flour
- 2 ½ tablespoons sugar
- 2 teaspoons bread machine yeast or active dry yeast

Directions:

1. Add water, butter, salt, and sugar to the bread machine pan.
2. Top with flour, then make a small well in the flour and add the yeast.
3. Select the Basic or White Bread cycle on your bread machine. Choose the crust color if your machine has this option.
4. After the cycle is finished, remove the bread from the pan and let it cool on a wire rack before slicing.

Nutritional per Serving: 150 calories, 4g protein, 27g carbohydrates, 2.5g fat, 1g fiber, 5mg cholesterol, 290mg sodium, 50mg potassium.

Tip: For a softer crust, wrap the bread in a clean cloth while it's still warm.

10. *Soft White Sandwich Bread*

Prep time: 10 minutes | Cook time: 3 hours

1 ½ Pounds Loaf (≈ 12 slices):

- 1 cup lukewarm water
- 2 tablespoons sugar
- 2 tablespoons unsalted butter, softened
- 1 ½ teaspoons salt
- 3 ¼ cups bread flour
- 1 ½ teaspoons bread machine yeast or active dry yeast

2 Pounds Loaf (≈ 16 slices):

- 1 ⅓ cups lukewarm water
- 2 ½ tablespoons sugar
- 3 tablespoons unsalted butter, softened
- 2 teaspoons salt
- 4 ⅓ cups bread flour
- 2 teaspoons bread machine yeast or active dry yeast

Directions:

1. Add water, sugar, butter, and salt to the bread machine pan.
2. Next, add the flour, ensuring it covers the liquid. Make a small indentation in the center of the flour and add the yeast.
3. Select the Basic or White Bread cycle on your bread machine. Choose the crust color if your machine has this feature.
4. After the baking cycle ends, remove the bread from the pan and let it cool on a wire rack before slicing.

Nutritional per Serving: 160 calories, 4g protein, 28g carbohydrates, 2.5g fat, 1g fiber, 5mg cholesterol, 290mg sodium, 50mg potassium.

Tip: For a softer crust, brush the top of the loaf with melted butter as soon as it comes out of the bread machine.

11. Chef's Crafted Sandwich

Prep time: 15 minutes | Cook time: 3 hours 15 minutes

1 ½ Pounds Loaf (≈ 12 slices):

- 1 cup + 2 tablespoons lukewarm water
- 2 tablespoons sugar
- 1 ½ teaspoons salt
- 2 tablespoons unsalted butter, melted
- 3 ¼ cups bread flour
- 1 ½ teaspoons bread machine yeast or active dry yeast
- ⅓ cup nonfat dry milk
- ½ cup instant mashed potato flakes

2 Pounds Loaf (≈ 16 slices):

- 1 ⅓ cups water, lukewarm water
- 2 ½ tablespoons sugar,
- 2 teaspoons salt
- 3 tablespoons unsalted butter, melted
- 4 ⅓ cups bread flour
- 2 teaspoons bread machine yeast or active dry yeast
- ½ cup nonfat dry milk
- ⅔ cup instant mashed potato flakes

Directions:

1. Place the water, sugar, melted butter, and salt in the bread machine pan.
2. Add the flour, nonfat dry milk, and instant mashed potato flakes on top, covering the liquid ingredients. Make a small indentation in the center of the dry ingredients and carefully place the yeast in it.
3. Select the Basic or White Bread cycle on your bread machine. Choose your preferred crust color if your machine has this option.
4. Once the cycle is complete, remove the bread from the pan and let it cool on a wire rack before slicing.

Nutritional per Serving: 180 calories, 5g protein, 34g carbohydrates, 2.5g fat, 1g fiber, 10mg cholesterol, 320mg sodium, 90mg potassium.

Tip: The addition of nonfat dry milk and instant mashed potato flakes gives the bread a tender texture and helps it stay fresh longer.

12. Honey Sandwich Bread

Prep time: 15 minutes | Cook time: 3 hours 30 minutes

1 ½ Pounds Loaf (≈ 12 slices):

- 1 cup + 1 tablespoon lukewarm water
- 2 tablespoons honey
- 1 tablespoon unsalted butter, softened
- 1 ½ teaspoons salt
- 3 cups bread flour
- 2 tablespoons dry milk powder
- 1 ½ teaspoons bread machine yeast or active dry yeast

2 Pounds Loaf (≈ 16 slices):

- 1 ⅓ cups lukewarm water
- 2 ½ tablespoons honey
- 1 ½ tablespoons unsalted butter, softened
- 2 teaspoons salt
- 4 cups bread flour
- 3 tablespoons dry milk powder
- 2 teaspoons bread machine yeast or active dry yeast

Directions:

1. Add the water, honey, butter, and salt to the bread machine pan.
2. Next, add the flour, milk powder, ensuring it covers the liquid. Make a small indentation in the center of the flour and add the yeast.
3. Select the Basic or White Bread cycle on your bread machine. Choose the crust color if your machine has this feature.
4. Once the baking cycle is complete, carefully remove the bread from the pan and let it cool on a wire rack before slicing.

Nutritional per Serving: 170 calories, 5g protein, 31g carbohydrates, 2g fat, 1g fiber, 5mg cholesterol, 300mg sodium, 80mg potassium.

Tip: Use high-quality honey for a rich flavor and a tender, aromatic crumb.

Chapter 4: Whole Grain Breads

A. Whole Wheat Bread Recipes

13. *Traditional Whole Wheat Loaf*

Prep time: 10 minutes | Cook time: 3 hours 30 minutes

1 ½ Pounds Loaf (≈ 12 slices):

- 1 cup + 2 tablespoons lukewarm water
- 2 tablespoons unsalted butter, melted
- 2 tablespoons molasses or honey
- 1 ½ teaspoons salt
- 2 cups whole wheat flour
- 1 ¼ cups bread flour
- 1 ½ teaspoons bread machine yeast or active dry yeast

2 Pounds Loaf (≈ 16 slices):

- 1 ⅓ cups water, lukewarm
- 3 tablespoons unsalted butter, melted
- 3 tablespoons molasses or honey
- 2 teaspoons salt
- 2 ⅔ cups whole wheat flour
- 1 ⅔ cups bread flour
- 2 teaspoons bread machine yeast or active dry yeast

Directions:

1. Add the water, butter, molasses (or honey), and salt to the bread machine pan.
2. Next, add the whole wheat flour and bread flour. Make a small indentation in the center of the flour and add the yeast.
3. Select the Whole Wheat Bread cycle on your bread machine. Choose the crust color if your machine has this feature.
4. Once the baking cycle is complete, carefully remove the bread from the pan and let it cool on a wire rack before slicing.

Nutritional per Serving: 160 calories, 5g protein, 30g carbohydrates, 2.5g fat, 4g fiber, 0mg cholesterol, 300mg sodium, 120mg potassium.

Tip: For a softer crust, wrap the loaf in a clean kitchen towel as it cools. This traps steam and keeps the crust soft.

14. *Honey Whole Wheat Bread*

Prep time: 10 minutes | Cook time: 3 hours 30 minutes

1 ½ Pounds Loaf (≈ 12 slices):

- 1 cup + 2 tablespoons lukewarm water
- ¼ cup honey
- 2 tablespoons unsalted butter, melted
- 1 ½ teaspoons salt
- 2 cups whole wheat flour
- 1 ¼ cups bread flour
- 1 ½ teaspoons bread machine yeast or active dry yeast

2 Pounds Loaf (≈ 16 slices):

- 1 ⅓ cups lukewarm water
- ⅓ cup honey
- 3 tablespoons unsalted butter, melted
- 2 teaspoons salt
- 2 ⅔ cups whole wheat flour
- 1 ⅔ cups bread flour
- 2 teaspoons bread machine yeast or active dry yeast

Directions:

1. Add the water, honey, butter, and salt to the bread machine pan.
2. Next, add the whole wheat flour and bread flour. Make a small indentation in the center of the flour and add the yeast.
3. Select the Whole Wheat Bread cycle on your bread machine. Choose the crust color if your machine has this feature.
4. Once the baking cycle is complete, carefully remove the bread from the pan and let it cool on a wire rack before slicing.

Nutritional per Serving: 180 calories, 6g protein, 34g carbohydrates, 3g fat, 4g fiber, 0mg cholesterol, 300mg sodium, 150mg potassium.

Tip: To ensure your honey integrates well, mix it with the lukewarm water before adding it to the bread machine.

15. *Whole Raisin & Walnut Bread*

Prep time: 15 minutes | Cook time: 3 hours 40 minutes

1 ½ Pounds Loaf (≈ 12 slices):

- 1 cup + 1 tablespoon lukewarm water
- 2 tablespoons honey
- 2 tablespoons vegetable oil
- 1 ½ teaspoons salt
- 1 ½ cups whole wheat flour
- 1 ½ cups bread flour
- ½ cup raisins
- ½ cup chopped walnuts
- 1 ½ teaspoons bread machine yeast or active dry yeast

2 Pounds Loaf (≈ 16 slices):

- 1 ⅓ cups lukewarm water
- 2 ½ tablespoons honey
- 3 tablespoons vegetable oil
- 2 teaspoons salt
- 2 cups whole wheat flour
- 2 cups bread flour
- ⅔ cup raisins
- ⅔ cup chopped walnuts
- 2 teaspoons bread machine yeast or active dry yeast

Directions:

1. Add the water, honey, oil, and salt to the bread machine pan.
2. Next, add the whole wheat flour and bread flour. Sprinkle the raisins and walnuts on top of the flour.
3. Make a small indentation in the center of the dry ingredients and add the yeast.
4. Select the Whole Wheat cycle on your bread machine and choose the crust color if your machine has this option.
5. Remove bread from pan after baking and cool on a wire rack before slicing.

Nutritional per Serving: 180 calories, 5g protein, 30g carbohydrates, 5g fat, 3g fiber, 0mg cholesterol, 300mg sodium, 100mg potassium.

Tip: Add raisins and walnuts after the first knead or at the machine's mix-in signal for even distribution.

16. *Whole Wheat & Oat Bread*

Prep time: 10 minutes | Cook time: 3 hours 30 minutes

1 ½ Pounds Loaf (≈ 12 slices):

- 1 cup + 2 tablespoons water, lukewarm
- 1 tablespoon honey or molasses
- 2 tablespoons vegetable oil
- 1 ½ teaspoons salt
- 1 ½ cups whole wheat flour
- 1 ½ cups bread flour
- ½ cup rolled oats
- 1 ½ teaspoons bread machine yeast or active dry yeast

2 Pounds Loaf (≈ 16 slices):

- 1 ⅓ cups water, lukewarm
- 2 tablespoons honey or molasses
- 3 tablespoons vegetable oil
- 2 teaspoons salt
- 2 cups whole wheat flour
- 2 cups bread flour
- ⅔ cup rolled oats
- 2 teaspoons bread machine yeast or active dry yeast

Directions:

1. Add water, honey (or molasses), oil, and salt to the bread machine pan.
2. Next, add the whole wheat flour, bread flour, and rolled oats. Make a small indentation in the center of the flour mixture and add the yeast.
3. Select the Whole Wheat Bread cycle on your bread machine. Choose the crust color if your machine has this feature.
4. After the cycle is complete, carefully remove the bread from the pan and let it cool on a wire rack before slicing.

Nutritional per Serving: 140 calories, 5g protein, 26g carbohydrates, 3g fat, 3g fiber, 0mg cholesterol, 300mg sodium, 100mg potassium.

Tip: To add a nutty flavor and extra nutrition, sprinkle a tablespoon of flaxseeds or sunflower seeds into the dough before the bread machine starts its kneading cycle.

B. Multigrain Bread Recipes

17. *Seven Grain Bread*

Prep time: 15 minutes | Cook time: 3 hours 40 minutes

1 ½ Pounds Loaf (≈ 12 slices):

- 1 cup + 2 tablespoons lukewarm water
- 2 tablespoons honey
- 2 tablespoons unsalted butter, melted
- 1 ½ teaspoons salt
- 2 cups seven-grain cereal mix
- 1 ½ cups bread flour
- 1 ½ teaspoons bread machine yeast or active dry yeast

2 Pounds Loaf (≈ 16 slices):

- 1 ⅓ cups lukewarm water
- 2 ½ tablespoons honey
- 3 tablespoons unsalted butter, melted
- 2 teaspoons salt
- 2 ⅔ cups seven-grain cereal mix
- 2 cups bread flour
- 2 teaspoons bread machine yeast or active dry yeast

Directions:

1. Add the water, honey, butter, and salt to the bread machine pan.
2. Next, add the seven-grain cereal mix and bread flour. Make a small indentation in the center of the flour and add the yeast.
3. Select the Grain Bread cycle on your bread machine. Choose the crust color if your machine has this feature.
4. Once the baking cycle is complete, carefully remove the bread from the pan and let it cool on a wire rack before slicing.

Nutritional per Serving: 180 calories, 6g protein, 32g carbohydrates, 3g fat, 4g fiber, 0mg cholesterol, 290mg sodium, 120mg potassium.

Tip: For a nuttier flavor and extra crunch, consider adding a tablespoon of mixed seeds (such as sunflower, sesame, or flax seeds) to the dough.

18. *Seeded Multigrain Bread*

Prep time: 15 minutes | Cook time: 3 hours 40 minutes

1 ½ Pounds Loaf (≈ 12 slices):

- 1 cup + 1 tablespoon lukewarm water
- ¼ cup honey or molasses
- 2 tablespoons unsalted butter, melted
- 1 ½ teaspoons salt
- 1 cup multigrain flour
- 2 cups bread flour
- ¼ cup mixed seeds (sunflower, pumpkin, flaxseed, etc.)
- 1 ½ teaspoons bread machine yeast or active dry yeast

2 Pounds Loaf (≈ 16 slices):

- 1 ⅓ cups lukewarm water
- ⅓ cup honey or molasses
- 3 tablespoons unsalted butter, melted
- 2 teaspoons salt
- 1 ⅓ cups multigrain flour
- 2 ⅔ cups bread flour
- ⅓ cup mixed seeds (sunflower, pumpkin, flaxseed, etc.)
- 2 teaspoons bread machine yeast or active dry yeast

Directions:

1. Add the water, honey (or molasses), butter, and salt to the bread machine pan.
2. Next, add the multigrain flour, bread flour, and mixed seeds. Make a small indentation in the center of the flour and add the yeast.
3. Select the Whole Wheat or Multigrain Bread cycle on your bread machine. Choose the crust color if your machine has this feature.
4. Once the baking cycle is complete, carefully remove the bread from the pan and let it cool on a wire rack before slicing.

Nutritional per Serving: 190 calories, 6g protein, 36g carbohydrates, 3g fat, 4g fiber, 0mg cholesterol, 300mg sodium, 130mg potassium.

Tip: For an extra crunchy crust and more flavor, sprinkle additional mixed seeds on top of the dough just before the baking cycle starts.

19. *Crunchy Seed and Grain Loaf*

Prep time: 15 minutes | Cook time: 3 hours 40 minutes

1 ½ Pounds Loaf (≈ 12 slices):

- 1 cup + 2 tablespoons lukewarm water
- 2 tablespoons honey or molasses
- 2 tablespoons unsalted butter, melted
- 1 ½ teaspoons salt
- 2 cups whole wheat flour
- 1 cup bread flour
- ¼ cup mixed seeds (sunflower, pumpkin, flaxseed, sesame)
- ¼ cup rolled oats
- 1 ½ teaspoons bread machine yeast or active dry yeast

2 Pounds Loaf (≈ 16 slices):

- 1 ⅓ cups lukewarm water
- 2 ½ tablespoons honey or molasses
- 3 tablespoons unsalted butter, melted
- 2 teaspoons salt
- 2 ⅔ cups whole wheat flour
- 1 ⅓ cups bread flour
- ⅓ cup mixed seeds (sunflower, pumpkin, flaxseed, sesame)
- ⅓ cup rolled oats
- 2 teaspoons bread machine yeast or active dry yeast

Directions:

1. Add water, honey (or molasses), butter, and salt to the bread machine pan.
2. Layer whole wheat flour, bread flour, seeds, and oats over liquid, make a well in the center, and add yeast.
3. Select the Whole Wheat or Grain cycle on your bread machine. Choose the crust color if your machine has this feature.
4. Remove bread from pan post-cycle and cool on a wire rack before slicing.

Nutritional per Serving: 180 calories, 6g protein, 32g carbohydrates, 4g fat, 3g fiber, 0mg cholesterol, 300mg sodium, 150mg potassium.

Tip: For added crunch, sprinkle seeds on the loaf before baking and mist with water to adhere.

20. *Harvest Multigrain Bread*

Prep time: 15 minutes | Cook time: 3 hours 40 minutes

1 ½ Pounds Loaf (≈ 12 slices):

- 1 cup + 1 tablespoon lukewarm water
- 2 tablespoons honey
- 2 tablespoons olive oil or melted unsalted butter
- 1 ½ teaspoons salt
- 1 cup multigrain cereal mix
- 2 cups bread flour
- 1 cup whole wheat flour
- 1 ½ teaspoons bread machine yeast or active dry yeast

2 Pounds Loaf (≈ 16 slices):

- 1 ⅓ cups lukewarm water
- 2 ½ tablespoons honey
- 2 ½ tablespoons olive oil or melted unsalted butter
- 2 teaspoons salt
- 1 ⅓ cups multigrain cereal mix
- 2 ⅔ cups bread flour
- 1 ⅓ cups whole wheat flour
- 2 teaspoons bread machine yeast or active dry yeast

Directions:

1. Add the water, honey, oil (or butter), and salt to the bread machine pan.
2. Next, add the multigrain cereal mix, bread flour, and whole wheat flour. Make a small indentation in the center of the flour and add the yeast.
3. Select the Whole Wheat or Grain Bread cycle on your bread machine. Choose the crust color if your machine has this feature.
4. Once the baking cycle is complete, carefully remove the bread from the pan and let it cool on a wire rack before slicing.

Nutritional per Serving: 170 calories, 6g protein, 33g carbohydrates, 2.5g fat, 4g fiber, 0mg cholesterol, 300mg sodium, 130mg potassium.

Tip: For extra texture and flavor, mix or sprinkle seeds like flax, sunflower, or pumpkin into/on dough before baking.

C. Rye Bread Recipes

21. *Classic Rye Bread*

Prep time: 15 minutes | Cook time: 3 hours 40 minutes

1 ½ Pounds Loaf (≈ 12 slices):

- 1 cup + 1 tablespoon lukewarm water
- 2 tablespoons molasses
- 1 tablespoon vegetable oil
- 1 ½ teaspoons salt
- 1 ½ cups rye flour
- 1 ¾ cups bread flour
- 2 teaspoons caraway seeds (optional)
- 1 ½ teaspoons bread machine yeast or active dry yeast

2 Pounds Loaf (≈ 16 slices):

- 1 ⅓ cups lukewarm water
- 2 ½ tablespoons molasses
- 1 ½ tablespoon vegetable oil
- 2 teaspoons salt
- 2 cups rye flour
- 2 ⅓ cups bread flour
- 1 tablespoon caraway seeds (optional)
- 2 teaspoons bread machine yeast or active dry yeast

Directions:

1. Add water, molasses, oil, and salt to the bread machine pan.
2. Next, add the rye flour, bread flour, and caraway seeds (if using). Make a small indentation in the center of the flour and add the yeast.
3. Select the Whole Wheat or Basic Bread cycle on your bread machine. Choose the crust color if your machine has this feature.
4. After the baking cycle is complete, remove the bread from the pan and let it cool on a wire rack before slicing.

Nutritional per Serving: 160 calories, 4g protein, 30g carbohydrates, 2g fat, 3g fiber, 0mg cholesterol, 300mg sodium, 80mg potassium.

Tip: For a more robust flavor, consider toasting the caraway seeds before adding them to the bread machine.

22. *Classic Caraway Rye Bread*

Prep time: 10 minutes | Cook time: 3 hours 40 minutes

1 ½ Pounds Loaf (≈ 12 slices):

- 1 cup + 1 tablespoon lukewarm water
- 1 ½ tablespoons molasses
- 1 tablespoon unsalted butter, softened
- 1 ½ teaspoons salt
- 1 ½ cups rye flour
- 1 ¾ cups bread flour
- 1 ½ tablespoons caraway seeds
- 1 ½ teaspoons bread machine yeast or active dry yeast

2 Pounds Loaf (≈ 16 slices):

- 1 ⅓ cups lukewarm water
- 2 tablespoons molasses
- 1 ½ tablespoons unsalted butter, softened
- 2 teaspoons salt
- 2 cups rye flour
- 2 ⅓ cups bread flour
- 2 tablespoons caraway seeds
- 2 teaspoons bread machine yeast or active dry yeast

Directions:

1. Add the water, molasses, butter, and salt to the bread machine pan.
2. Next, add the rye flour, bread flour, and caraway seeds. Make a small indentation in the center of the flour and add the yeast.
3. Select the Rye Bread cycle on your bread machine. Choose the crust color if your machine has this feature.
4. Once the baking cycle is complete, carefully remove the bread from the pan and let it cool on a wire rack before slicing.

Nutritional per Serving: 160 calories, 5g protein, 32g carbohydrates, 2g fat, 3g fiber, 0mg cholesterol, 300mg sodium, 80mg potassium.

Tip: For a stronger caraway flavor, lightly toast the seeds before adding them to the mix.

23. Dark Rye Bread

Prep time: 10 minutes | Cook time: 3 hours 40 minutes

1 ½ Pounds Loaf (≈ 12 slices):

- 1 cup + 2 tablespoons lukewarm water
- 2 tablespoons molasses
- 1 tablespoon unsalted butter, softened
- 1 ½ teaspoons salt
- 1 ½ cups rye flour
- 1 ¾ cups bread flour
- 2 tablespoons unsweetened cocoa powder
- 1 ½ teaspoons bread machine yeast or active dry yeast

2 Pounds Loaf (≈ 16 slices):

- 1 ⅓ cups lukewarm water
- 2 ½ tablespoons molasses
- 1 ½ tablespoon unsalted butter, softened
- 2 teaspoons salt
- 2 cups rye flour
- 2 ⅓ cups bread flour
- 2 ½ tablespoons unsweetened cocoa powder
- 2 teaspoons bread machine yeast or active dry yeast

Directions:

1. Place water, molasses, butter, and salt in the bread machine pan.
2. Add rye flour, bread flour, and cocoa powder on top. Make a small well in the flour and add the yeast.
3. Select the Whole Wheat or Dark Bread cycle on your bread machine. Choose the crust color if your machine has this feature.
4. After the baking cycle is complete, carefully remove the bread from the pan and let it cool on a wire rack before slicing.

Nutritional per Serving: 160 calories, 4g protein, 30g carbohydrates, 2g fat, 3g fiber, 5mg cholesterol, 290mg sodium, 100mg potassium.

Tip: For a deeper flavor, toast the rye flour lightly before using.

24. Marble Rye Swirl

Prep time: 20 minutes | Cook time: 3 hours 40 minutes

1 ½ Pounds Loaf (≈ 12 slices):

- 1 cup + 2 tablespoons lukewarm water
- 1 ½ tablespoons molasses
- 1 tablespoon unsalted butter, softened
- 1 ½ teaspoons salt
- 1 cup rye flour
- 2 ¼ cups bread flour
- 1 ½ teaspoons bread machine yeast or active dry yeast
- 1 tablespoon cocoa powder (for half of the dough)

2 Pounds Loaf (≈ 16 slices):

- 1 ⅓ cups lukewarm water
- 2 tablespoons molasses
- 1 ½ tablespoon unsalted butter, softened
- 2 teaspoons salt
- 1 ⅓ cups rye flour
- 3 cups bread flour
- 2 teaspoons bread machine yeast or active dry yeast
- 1 ½ tablespoons cocoa powder (for half of the dough)

Directions:

1. Halve ingredients for two doughs: plain rye and dark rye (add cocoa to dark rye).
2. For each dough, add to the machine in this order: water, molasses, butter, salt, flour, yeast on top.
3. Run dough cycle separately. After, roll out each dough, layer dark rye on plain rye, and roll together tightly.
4. Put rolled dough in machine, select Basic cycle and crust preference.
5. After baking, cool bread on a wire rack before slicing.

Nutritional per Serving: 160 calories, 5g protein, 31g carbohydrates, 2g fat, 3g fiber, 0mg cholesterol, 290mg sodium, 110mg potassium.

Tip: For a well-defined swirl, roll the doughs together tightly and seal the edges well before the final rise.

Chapter 5: Spice, Herb, and Vegetable Breads

A. Spice-Infused Bread Recipes

25. Cardamom Bread

Prep time: 15 minutes | Cook time: 3 hours

1 ½ Pounds Loaf (≈ 12 slices):

- 1 cup + 2 tablespoons lukewarm milk
- 2 tablespoons unsalted butter, melted
- 3 tablespoons sugar
- 1 ½ teaspoons ground cardamom
- ½ teaspoon salt
- 3 ¼ cups bread flour
- 1 ½ teaspoons bread machine yeast or active dry yeast

2 Pounds Loaf (≈ 16 slices):

- 1 ⅓ cups lukewarm milk
- 3 tablespoons unsalted butter, melted
- ¼ cup sugar
- 2 teaspoons ground cardamom
- ¾ teaspoon salt
- 4 ⅓ cups bread flour
- 2 teaspoons bread machine yeast or active dry yeast

Directions:

1. Place the milk, melted butter, sugar, ground cardamom, and salt in the bread machine pan.
2. Add the flour, covering the liquid ingredients. Make a small indentation in the center of the flour and carefully place the yeast in it.
3. Select the Basic or White Bread cycle on your bread machine. Choose your preferred crust color if your machine has this option.
4. Once the baking cycle is complete, remove the bread from the pan and let it cool on a wire rack before slicing.

Nutritional per Serving: 180 calories, 6g protein, 33g carbohydrates, 3g fat, 1g fiber, 10mg cholesterol, 125mg sodium, 80mg potassium.

Tip: Ensure your cardamom is freshly ground for the most aromatic results.

26. Cinnamon Raisin Bread

Prep time: 15 minutes | Cook time: 3 hours 30 minutes

1 ½ Pounds Loaf (≈ 12 slices):

- 1 cup + 2 tablespoons lukewarm water
- 3 tablespoons sugar
- 2 tablespoons unsalted butter, softened
- 1 ½ teaspoons cinnamon
- 1 ½ teaspoons salt
- 3 ¼ cups bread flour
- ⅔ cup raisins
- 1 ½ teaspoons bread machine yeast or active dry yeast

2 Pounds Loaf (≈ 16 slices):

- 1 ⅓ cups lukewarm water
- ¼ cup sugar
- 3 tablespoons unsalted butter, softened
- 2 teaspoons cinnamon
- 2 teaspoons salt
- 4 ⅓ cups bread flour
- 1 cup raisins
- 2 teaspoons bread machine yeast or active dry yeast

Directions:

1. Add the water, sugar, butter, cinnamon, and salt to the bread machine pan.
2. Next, add the flour. Make a small indentation in the center of the flour and add the yeast. Sprinkle the raisins on top of the flour.
3. Select the Sweet Bread cycle on your bread machine. Choose the crust color if your machine has this feature.
4. Once the baking cycle is complete, carefully remove the bread from the pan and let it cool on a wire rack before slicing.

Nutritional per Serving: 200 calories, 5g protein, 40g carbohydrates, 2.5g fat, 2g fiber, 0mg cholesterol, 300mg sodium, 100mg potassium.

Tip: For best distribution, add the raisins at the beep or during the raisin/nut cycle if your machine has one.

27. Chai Spice Bread

Prep time: 10 minutes | Cook time: 3 hours 30 minutes

1 ½ Pounds Loaf (≈ 12 slices):

- 1 cup + 2 tablespoons lukewarm water
- 2 tablespoons vegetable oil
- 2 tablespoons sugar
- 1 teaspoon salt
- 3 cups bread flour
- 1 ½ teaspoons chai spice mix (blend of ground cinnamon, cardamom, ginger, allspice, and cloves)
- 2 teaspoons active dry yeast

2 Pounds Loaf (≈ 16 slices):

- 1 ⅓ cups lukewarm water
- 3 tablespoons vegetable oil
- 3 tablespoons sugar
- 1 ¼ teaspoons salt
- 4 cups bread flour
- 2 teaspoons chai spice mix (blend of ground cinnamon, cardamom, ginger, allspice, and cloves)
- 2 ½ teaspoons active dry yeast

Directions:

1. Add the water, vegetable oil, sugar, and salt to the bread machine pan. Next, add the bread flour, ensuring it covers the liquid. On top of the flour, add the chai spice mix. Make a small indentation on top of the dry ingredients (but not deep enough to reach the liquid) and add the yeast into this indentation.
2. Set your bread machine to the basic or white bread setting with a medium crust.
3. Once the baking cycle is complete, carefully remove the bread from the pan and allow it to cool on a wire rack before slicing.

Nutritional per Serving: 190 calories, 5g protein, 36g carbohydrates, 3g fat, 1g fiber, 10mg cholesterol, 200mg sodium, 80mg potassium.

Tip: Brush top with milk and a pinch of chai spice pre-final rise for a flavorful crust.

28. Pumpkin Spice Bread

Prep time: 15 minutes | Cook time: 3 hours 40 minutes

1 ½ Pounds Loaf (≈ 12 slices):

- ⅔ cup canned pumpkin puree
- ¼ cup water
- 2 tablespoons vegetable oil
- 3 tablespoons brown sugar
- 1 teaspoon salt
- 3 cups bread flour
- 1 ½ teaspoons pumpkin pie spice (blend of ground cinnamon, ginger, nutmeg, and cloves)
- 2 teaspoons active dry yeast

2 Pounds Loaf (≈ 16 slices):

- 1 cup canned pumpkin puree
- ⅓ cup water
- 3 tablespoons vegetable oil
- ¼ cup brown sugar
- 1 ¼ teaspoons salt
- 4 cups bread flour
- 2 teaspoons pumpkin pie spice (blend of ground cinnamon, ginger, nutmeg, and cloves)
- 2 ½ teaspoons active dry yeast

Directions:

1. Place pumpkin, water, butter, and sugar in the bread machine pan. Then add the salt.
2. Carefully add the bread flour over the wet ingredients, ensuring to cover them completely. Sprinkle the pumpkin pie spice evenly over the flour. Make a small indentation on top of the flour (without reaching the wet mixture) and add the yeast to this indentation.
3. Set your bread machine to the basic or white bread cycle with a medium crust setting.
4. After baking, remove the bread and cool on a rack before slicing.

Nutritional per Serving: 190 calories, 5g protein, 36g carbohydrates, 3g fat, 1g fiber, 10mg cholesterol, 200mg sodium, 80mg potassium.

Tip: Brush top with milk and a pinch of chai spice pre-final rise for a flavorful crust.

B. Herb-Enhanced Bread Recipes

29. *Rosemary Olive Bread*

Prep time: 15 minutes | Cook time: 3 hours 40 minutes

1 ½ Pounds Loaf (≈ 12 slices):

- 1 cup + 2 tablespoons lukewarm water
- 2 tablespoons olive oil
- 3 cups bread flour
- 1 ½ teaspoons salt
- 2 tablespoons sugar
- 2 tablespoons fresh rosemary, chopped
- ½ cup black olives, pitted and chopped
- 2 teaspoons active dry yeast

2 Pounds Loaf (≈ 16 slices):

- 1 ⅓ cups lukewarm water
- 3 tablespoons olive oil
- 4 cups bread flour
- 2 teaspoons salt
- 2 ½ tablespoons sugar
- 2 ½ tablespoons fresh rosemary, chopped
- ⅔ cup black olives, pitted and chopped
- 2 ½ teaspoons active dry yeast

Directions:

1. Add water and olive oil into the bread machine pan. Then, add the bread flour, ensuring it spreads evenly over the liquid. Sprinkle the salt and sugar over the flour.
2. Add the chopped rosemary and olives on top of the flour. Make a small indentation in the center of the flour mixture and carefully add the yeast to this indentation.
3. Select the basic or white bread cycle on your bread machine and choose the medium crust setting.
4. After the bread has finished baking, carefully remove it from the pan and let it cool on a wire rack before slicing.

Nutritional per Serving: 180 calories, 5g protein, 33g carbohydrates, 4g fat, 2g fiber, 0mg cholesterol, 400mg sodium, 50mg potassium.

Tip: For a crisper crust, remove the bread from the machine after the baking cycle and finish it in a preheated 375°F oven for 10-15 minutes.

30. *Italian Herb Bread*

Prep time: 15 minutes | Cook time: 3 hours 40 minutes

1 ½ Pounds Loaf (≈ 12 slices):

- 1 cup lukewarm water
- 2 tablespoons olive oil
- 3 cups bread flour
- 1 ½ teaspoons salt
- 1 tablespoon sugar
- 2 teaspoons Italian seasoning (blend of dried basil, oregano, rosemary, thyme)
- 2 tablespoons grated Parmesan cheese
- 2 teaspoons active dry yeast

2 Pounds Loaf (≈ 16 slices):

- 1 ¼ cups lukewarm water
- 3 tablespoons olive oil
- 4 cups bread flour
- 2 teaspoons salt
- 1 ½ tablespoons sugar
- 2 ½ teaspoons Italian seasoning (blend of dried basil, oregano, rosemary, thyme)
- 3 tablespoons grated Parmesan cheese
- 2 ½ teaspoons active dry yeast

Directions:

1. Pour water and olive oil into the bread machine pan. Next, add the bread flour, ensuring it completely covers the liquid. Sprinkle the salt, sugar, Italian seasoning, and grated Parmesan cheese on top of the flour.
2. Make a small indentation in the center of the flour mixture without reaching the liquid. Add the yeast to this indentation.
3. Select the basic or white bread cycle on your bread machine and adjust the crust setting to medium.
4. After baking, remove the bread and cool on a rack before slicing.

Nutritional per Serving: 190 calories, 6g protein, 34g carbohydrates, 4g fat, 1g fiber, 1mg cholesterol, 390mg sodium, 60mg potassium.

Tip: Brush the top of the dough with olive oil and sprinkle with a bit more Italian seasoning before the final rise for an extra flavorful crust.

31. Dill Onion Bread

Prep time: 10 minutes | Cook time: 3 hours 35 minutes

1 ½ Pounds Loaf (≈ 12 slices):

- 1 cup + 1 tablespoon lukewarm water
- 2 tablespoons olive oil
- 3 cups bread flour
- 1 tablespoon sugar
- 1 ½ teaspoons salt
- ¼ cup dried minced onion
- 2 tablespoons fresh dill, chopped (or 2 teaspoons dried dill weed)
- 2 teaspoons active dry yeast

2 Pounds Loaf (≈ 16 slices):

- 1 ⅓ cups lukewarm water
- 3 tablespoons olive oil
- 4 cups bread flour
- 1 ½ tablespoons sugar
- 2 teaspoons salt
- ⅓ cup dried minced onion
- 3 tablespoons fresh dill, chopped (or 1 tablespoon dried dill weed)
- 2 ½ teaspoons active dry yeast

Directions:

1. Add the water and olive oil to the bread machine pan. Follow this with the bread flour, making sure it covers the liquid completely. Add the sugar and salt evenly over the flour.
2. Sprinkle the dried minced onion and dill over the top of the flour mixture. Make a small indentation in the center of the flour (but not deep enough to reach the liquid) and add the yeast to this indentation.
3. Select the basic or white bread setting on your bread machine, with a medium crust preference.
4. After baking, carefully remove the bread and cool on a rack before slicing.

Nutritional per Serving: 180 calories, 5g protein, 35g carbohydrates, 3g fat, 1g fiber, 0mg cholesterol, 300mg sodium, 80mg potassium.

Tip: For a more intense flavor, soak the dried minced onion in the measured water for about 10 minutes before adding to the bread machine.

32. Basil Pesto Bread

Prep time: 15 minutes | Cook time: 3 hours 50 minutes

1 ½ Pounds Loaf (≈ 12 slices):

- 1 cup lukewarm water
- 2 tablespoons olive oil
- 3 cups bread flour
- 1 ½ teaspoons salt
- 2 tablespoons sugar
- ¼ cup basil pesto
- 2 teaspoons active dry yeast

2 Pounds Loaf (≈ 16 slices):

- 1 ⅓ cups lukewarm water
- 3 tablespoons olive oil
- 4 cups bread flour
- 2 teaspoons salt
- 2 ½ tablespoons sugar
- ⅓ cup basil pesto
- 2 ½ teaspoons active dry yeast

Directions:

1. Pour the water and olive oil into the bread machine pan. Then add the bread flour, ensuring that it completely covers the liquid. Evenly sprinkle the salt and sugar over the flour.
2. Add the basil pesto on top of the flour mixture. Make a small indentation in the center of the flour (but not deep enough to reach the liquid) and add the yeast to this indentation.
3. Select the basic or white bread cycle on your bread machine and choose the medium crust option.
4. Once the bread cycle has completed, carefully remove the bread from the machine and let it cool on a wire rack before slicing.

Nutritional per Serving: 190 calories, 6g protein, 35g carbohydrates, 4g fat, 1g fiber, 5mg cholesterol, 400mg sodium, 50mg potassium.

Tip: For an extra burst of flavor, add a tablespoon of freshly grated Parmesan cheese to the dough before the final kneading cycle.

C. Vegetable Bread Recipes

33. *Tomato Basil Bread*

Prep time: 10 minutes | Cook time: 3 hours 40 minutes

1 ½ Pounds Loaf (≈ 12 slices):

- ¾ cup tomato juice (at room temperature)
- 2 tablespoons olive oil
- 3 cups bread flour
- 1 tablespoon sugar
- 1 ½ teaspoons salt
- 2 tablespoons fresh basil, chopped (or 2 teaspoons dried basil)
- 2 teaspoons active dry yeast

2 Pounds Loaf (≈ 16 slices):

- 1 cup tomato juice (at room temperature)
- 3 tablespoons olive oil
- 4 cups bread flour
- 1 ½ tablespoons sugar
- 2 teaspoons salt
- 3 tablespoons fresh basil, chopped (or 1 tablespoon dried basil)
- 2 ½ teaspoons active dry yeast

Directions:

1. Add the tomato juice and olive oil into the bread machine pan.
2. Over this, add the bread flour, making sure to cover the liquid. Then, evenly distribute the sugar and salt across the flour.
3. Sprinkle the chopped basil over the top. Make a small indentation in the middle of the flour (but not deep enough to reach the liquid) and add the yeast to this indentation.
4. Select the basic or white bread cycle on your bread machine and adjust the crust setting to medium.
5. Once done, remove the bread from the machine and let it cool before slicing.

Nutritional per Serving: 185 calories, 5g protein, 35g carbohydrates, 3g fat, 1g fiber, 0mg cholesterol, 300mg sodium, 100mg potassium.

Tip: For a richer tomato flavor, consider using a tomato juice that's low in sodium and high in natural flavors.

34. *Carrot Bread*

Prep time: 15 minutes | Cook time: 3 hours 30 minutes

1 ½ Pounds Loaf (≈ 12 slices):

- ¾ cup finely grated carrot
- 1 cup lukewarm water
- 2 tablespoons vegetable oil
- 3 cups bread flour
- 2 tablespoons sugar
- 1 teaspoon salt
- 1 ½ teaspoons cinnamon
- 2 teaspoons active dry yeast

2 Pounds Loaf (≈ 16 slices):

- 1 cup finely grated carrot
- 1 ⅓ cups lukewarm water
- 3 tablespoons vegetable oil
- 4 cups bread flour
- 2 ½ tablespoons sugar
- 1 ¼ teaspoons salt
- 2 teaspoons cinnamon
- 2 ½ teaspoons active dry yeast

Directions:

1. Prepare carrots: wash, peel, finely grate, then measure the needed amount.
2. In the bread machine pan, add water, vegetable oil, then grated carrot.
3. Add the bread flour, ensuring to completely cover the wet ingredients. Sprinkle the sugar, salt, and cinnamon evenly over the flour.
4. Make a small indentation in the center of the flour mixture (but not deep enough to reach the liquid) and add the yeast to this indentation.
5. Select the basic or white bread cycle on your bread machine, and choose the medium crust setting.
6. Once done, remove the bread from the machine and let it cool before slicing.

Nutritional per Serving: 175 calories, 5g protein, 33g carbohydrates, 2g fat, 1g fiber, 0mg cholesterol, 200mg sodium, 80mg potassium.

Tip: For sweetness and texture, add a quarter cup of raisins or chopped walnuts before the final knead.

35. Zucchini Bread

Prep time: 20 minutes | Cook time: 3 hours 40 minutes

1 ½ Pounds Loaf (≈ 12 slices):

- ¾ cup grated zucchini, moisture squeezed out
- 1 cup lukewarm water
- 2 tablespoons olive oil
- 3 cups bread flour
- 1 teaspoon salt
- 2 tablespoons sugar
- 1 ½ teaspoons cinnamon
- ½ teaspoon nutmeg
- 2 teaspoons active dry yeast

2 Pounds Loaf (≈ 16 slices):

- 1 cup grated zucchini, moisture squeezed out
- 1 ⅓ cups lukewarm water
- 3 tablespoons olive oil
- 4 cups bread flour
- 1 ¼ teaspoons salt
- 2 ½ tablespoons sugar
- 2 teaspoons cinnamon
- ¾ teaspoon nutmeg
- 2 ½ teaspoons active dry yeast

Directions:

1. Shred zucchini, wrap in a towel, and squeeze to remove moisture.
2. Pour the water and olive oil into the bread machine pan. Add the drained zucchini.
3. Cover wet ingredients with bread flour, then evenly sprinkle salt, sugar, cinnamon, nutmeg.
4. Make a small indentation in the center of the flour mixture (without reaching the wet ingredients) and add the yeast to this indentation.
5. Select the basic or white bread cycle on your bread machine, and adjust the crust setting to medium.
6. Once done, carefully remove the bread from the machine and let it cool before slicing.

Nutritional per Serving: 180 calories, 5g protein, 35g carbohydrates, 3g fat, 1g fiber, 0mg cholesterol, 200mg sodium, 90mg potassium.

Tip: For added texture and nutrition, stir in a quarter cup of chopped walnuts or pecans into the batter before starting the bread machine.

36. Pumpkin Bread

Prep time: 15 minutes | Cook time: 3 hours 45 minutes

1 ½ Pounds Loaf (≈ 12 slices):

- ⅔ cup pumpkin puree (not pumpkin pie filling)
- ½ cup lukewarm water
- 2 tablespoons vegetable oil
- 3 cups bread flour
- 2 tablespoons sugar
- 1 teaspoon salt
- 1 ½ teaspoons pumpkin pie spice (blend of cinnamon, ginger, nutmeg, and cloves)
- 2 teaspoons active dry yeast

2 Pounds Loaf (≈ 16 slices):

- 1 cup pumpkin puree (not pumpkin pie filling)
- ⅔ cup water
- 3 tablespoons vegetable oil
- 4 cups bread flour
- 3 tablespoons sugar
- 1 ¼ teaspoons salt
- 2 teaspoons pumpkin pie spice (blend of cinnamon, ginger, nutmeg, and cloves)
- 2 ½ teaspoons active dry yeast

Directions:

1. Add the pumpkin puree, water, and vegetable oil to the bread machine pan.
2. Add bread flour to fully cover liquid ingredients, then evenly sprinkle sugar, salt, and pumpkin pie spice over it.
3. Make a small indentation in the center of the flour mixture (but not deep enough to reach the liquid) and add the yeast to this indentation.
4. Select the basic or white bread cycle on your bread machine, adjusting the crust setting to medium.
5. Once done, carefully remove the bread from the machine and let it cool before slicing.

Nutritional per Serving: 180 calories, 5g protein, 34g carbohydrates, 3g fat, 1g fiber, 0mg cholesterol, 200mg sodium, 90mg potassium.

Tip: For sweetness and texture, add a handful of dried cranberries or chopped walnuts to the dough before the final kneading cycle.

Chapter 6: Breakfast Breads

A. Sweet Bread Recipes

37. Chocolate Chip Bread

Prep time: 10 minutes | Cook time: 3 hours 30 minutes

1 ½ Pounds Loaf (≈ 12 slices):

- 1 cup lukewarm water
- 2 tablespoons unsalted butter, softened
- 3 cups bread flour
- 2 tablespoons sugar
- 1 teaspoon salt
- 2 teaspoons active dry yeast
- ½ cup semisweet chocolate chips

2 Pounds Loaf (≈ 16 slices):

- 1 ⅓ cups lukewarm water
- 3 tablespoons unsalted butter, softened
- 4 cups bread flour
- 3 tablespoons sugar
- 1 ¼ teaspoons salt
- 2 ½ teaspoons active dry yeast
- ⅔ cup semisweet chocolate chips

Directions:

1. Add water and softened butter into the bread machine pan. Over this, add the bread flour, making sure to cover the liquid entirely. Then evenly sprinkle the sugar and salt over the flour.
2. Make a small indentation in the center of the flour mixture and add the yeast to this indentation.
3. Select the sweet, basic or white Bread cycle, and adjust the crust to your preferred setting.
4. Just before the final kneading cycle ends add the chocolate chips. This prevents them from melting completely during the mixing process.
5. Once done, carefully remove the bread from the machine and let it cool before slicing.

Nutritional per Serving: 210 calories, 5g protein, 38g carbohydrates, 5g fat, 2g fiber, 8mg cholesterol, 200mg sodium, 90mg potassium.

Tip: Ideally, use high-quality chocolate chips to ensure they maintain their shape and provide a rich chocolate flavor throughout the bread.

38. Honey Almond Bread

Prep time: 15 minutes | Cook time: 3 hours 40 minutes

1 ½ Pounds Loaf (≈ 12 slices):

- 1 cup + 1 tablespoon lukewarm water
- 2 tablespoons honey
- 2 tablespoons unsalted butter, softened
- 3 cups bread flour
- 2 tablespoons dry milk powder
- 1 teaspoon salt
- 2 teaspoons active dry yeast
- ½ cup sliced almonds

2 Pounds Loaf (≈ 16 slices):

- 1 ⅓ cups lukewarm water
- 3 tablespoons honey
- 3 tablespoons unsalted butter, softened
- 4 cups bread flour
- 2 ½ tablespoons dry milk powder
- 1 ¼ teaspoons salt
- 2 ½ teaspoons active dry yeast
- ⅔ cup sliced almonds

Directions:

1. Place the water, honey, and softened butter into the bread machine pan. Then add the bread flour, covering the liquid. Sprinkle the dry milk powder and salt evenly over the flour.
2. Make a small well in the center of the flour and add the yeast.
3. Select the sweet, basic or white Bread cycle, and adjust the crust to your preferred setting.
4. Add the sliced almonds about 5 minutes before the last kneading cycle ends.
5. Once done, remove the bread from the machine and let it cool before slicing.

Nutritional per Serving: 210 calories, 6g protein, 37g carbohydrates, 5g fat, 2g fiber, 10mg cholesterol, 200mg sodium, 100mg potassium.

Tip: To enhance the almond flavor, consider adding a few drops of almond extract along with the honey.

39. Vanilla Bean Bread

Prep time: 15 minutes | Cook time: 3 hours 30 minutes

1 ½ Pounds Loaf (≈ 12 slices):

- 1 cup milk, warmed to about 80°F
- 2 tablespoons unsalted butter, softened
- 1 vanilla bean, split and scraped (or 1 teaspoon vanilla extract)
- 3 cups bread flour
- 2 tablespoons sugar
- 1 teaspoon salt
- 2 teaspoons active dry yeast

2 Pounds Loaf (≈ 16 slices):

- 1 ⅓ cups milk, warmed to about 80°F
- 3 tablespoons unsalted butter, softened
- 1 large vanilla bean, split and scraped (or 1 ½ teaspoons vanilla extract)
- 4 cups bread flour
- 3 tablespoons sugar
- 1 ¼ teaspoons salt
- 2 ½ teaspoons active dry yeast

Directions:

1. Add the warmed milk and softened butter to the bread machine pan. If using a vanilla bean, scrape the seeds from the pod and add them to the pan (or add vanilla extract).
2. Over this, add the bread flour, ensuring to cover the liquid ingredients. Then evenly sprinkle the sugar and salt over the flour.
3. Make a small indentation in the center of the flour mixture (but not deep enough to reach the liquid) and add the yeast to this indentation.
4. Select the sweet, basic or white bread cycle on your bread machine, and adjust the crust to your preferred setting.
5. Once the baking cycle is complete, carefully remove the bread from the pan and let it cool on a wire rack before slicing.

Nutritional per Serving: 180 calories, 5g protein, 34g carbohydrates, 3g fat, 1g fiber, 10mg cholesterol, 200mg sodium, 80mg potassium.

Tip: Enhance the vanilla flavor by brushing the top of the bread with a little melted butter and sprinkling with sugar just before the final rise.

40. Cinnamon Swirl Bread

Prep time: 20 minutes | Cook time: 3 hours 50 minutes

1 ½ Pounds Loaf (≈ 12 slices):

- 1 cup + 1 tablespoon milk, at room temperature
- 2 tablespoons unsalted butter, softened
- 3 cups bread flour
- 2 tablespoons sugar
- 1 teaspoon salt
- 2 teaspoons active dry yeast
- 2 tablespoons unsalted butter, melted
- ¼ cup sugar and 1 tablespoon cinnamon

2 Pounds Loaf (≈ 16 slices):

- 1 ⅓ cups milk, at room temperature
- 3 tablespoons unsalted butter, softened
- 4 cups bread flour
- 3 tablespoons sugar
- 1 ¼ teaspoons salt
- 2 ½ teaspoons active dry yeast
- 3 tablespoons unsalted butter, melted
- ⅓ cup sugar and 1 ½ tablespoons cinnamon

Directions:

1. Place milk and softened butter in the bread machine pan. Add bread flour, ensuring it covers the liquid. Sprinkle sugar and salt over the flour. Make a small indentation in the flour for the yeast and add it.
2. Select the dough cycle on your bread machine.
3. Once the dough cycle is complete, roll out the dough on a lightly floured surface into a rectangle. Brush with melted butter, and sprinkle with a mix of sugar and cinnamon.
4. Roll the dough tightly from the long end, pinch the seams to seal, and place it back into the bread machine pan. Select the bake cycle or use the sweet/basic/white bread setting to bake.
5. Once done, carefully remove the bread from the machine and let it cool before slicing.

Nutritional per Serving: 190 calories, 5g protein, 35g carbohydrates, 4g fat, 1g fiber, 10mg cholesterol, 200mg sodium, 80mg potassium.

Tip: For a more pronounced swirl, avoid pressing down too hard when rolling up the dough with the cinnamon sugar to ensure the layers remain distinct.

B. Savory Bread Recipes

41. *Garlic Herb Bread*

Prep time: 10 minutes | Cook time: 3 hours 35 minutes

1 ½ Pounds Loaf (≈ 12 slices):

- 1 cup lukewarm water
- 2 tablespoons olive oil
- 3 cups bread flour
- 1 tablespoon sugar
- 1 teaspoon salt
- 2 teaspoons garlic powder
- 1 tablespoon dried Italian herbs (a blend of oregano, basil, rosemary, thyme)
- 2 teaspoons active dry yeast

2 Pounds Loaf (≈ 16 slices):

- 1 ⅓ cups water
- 3 tablespoons olive oil
- 4 cups bread flour
- 1 ½ tablespoons sugar
- 1 ¼ teaspoons salt
- 2 ½ teaspoons garlic powder
- 1 ½ tablespoons dried Italian herbs (a blend of oregano, basil, rosemary, thyme)
- 2 ½ teaspoons active dry yeast

Directions:

1. Pour water and olive oil into the bread machine pan then add the bread flour, ensuring it completely covers the liquid. Sprinkle the sugar, salt, garlic powder, and dried Italian herbs over the flour.
2. Make a small indentation in the center of the flour mixture and add the yeast to this indentation.
3. Select the basic or white bread setting on your bread machine, and adjust the crust to your preferred setting.
4. Once done, remove the bread from the machine and let it cool before slicing.

Nutritional per Serving: 190 calories, 6g protein, 35g carbohydrates, 3g fat, 2g fiber, 0mg cholesterol, 200mg sodium, 100mg potassium.

Tip: For a more intense flavor, you can add a tablespoon of freshly grated Parmesan cheese to the dough before the final kneading cycle.

42. *Onion and Poppy Seed Bread*

Prep time: 10 minutes | Cook time: 3 hours 30 minutes

1 ½ Pounds Loaf (≈ 12 slices):

- 1 cup + 2 tablespoons lukewarm water
- 2 tablespoons vegetable oil
- 3 cups bread flour
- 2 tablespoons dry milk powder
- 1 tablespoon sugar
- 1 ½ teaspoons salt
- 2 tablespoons dried minced onion
- 2 tablespoons poppy seeds
- 2 teaspoons active dry yeast

2 Pounds Loaf (≈ 16 slices):

- 1 ⅓ cups lukewarm water
- 3 tablespoons vegetable oil
- 4 cups bread flour
- 2 ½ tablespoons dry milk powder
- 1 ½ tablespoons sugar
- 2 teaspoons salt
- 3 tablespoons dried minced onion
- 3 tablespoons poppy seeds
- 2 ½ teaspoons active dry yeast

Directions:

1. Pour water and vegetable oil into the bread machine pan. Then add the bread flour, ensuring it completely covers the liquid. Then, evenly distribute the dry milk powder, sugar, and salt over the flour.
2. Sprinkle the dried minced onion and poppy seeds on top of the flour mixture.
3. Make a small well in the center of the flour (without reaching the liquid) and add the yeast to this well.
4. Select the basic or white bread setting on your bread machine, and adjust the crust to your preferred setting.
5. Once done, remove the bread from the machine and let it cool before slicing.

Nutritional per Serving: 180 calories, 5g protein, 34g carbohydrates, 3g fat, 2g fiber, 0mg cholesterol, 300mg sodium, 100mg potassium.

Tip: Toasting slices of this bread enhances the flavors of the onion and poppy seeds, making for a delicious breakfast option or sandwich base.

43. Sun-Dried Tomato Bread

Prep time: 15 minutes | Cook time: 3 hours 40 minutes

1 ½ Pounds Loaf (≈ 12 slices):

- 1 cup lukewarm water
- 2 tablespoons olive oil
- 3 cups bread flour
- 2 tablespoons sugar
- 1 teaspoon salt
- ⅓ cup sun-dried tomatoes, chopped (not in oil)
- 1 tablespoon dried basil
- 2 teaspoons active dry yeast

2 Pounds Loaf (≈ 16 slices):

- 1 ⅓ cups water
- 3 tablespoons olive oil
- 4 cups bread flour
- 2 ½ tablespoons sugar
- 1 ¼ teaspoons salt
- ½ cup sun-dried tomatoes, chopped not in oil
- 1 ½ tablespoons dried basil
- 2 ½ teaspoons active dry yeast

Directions:

1. Add the water and olive oil into the bread machine pan. Then add the bread flour on top, making sure it completely covers the liquid. Sprinkle the sugar and salt evenly over the flour.
2. Distribute the chopped sun-dried tomatoes and dried basil over the flour. Make a small well in the center of the flour (without reaching the liquid) and add the yeast to this well.
3. Select the basic or white bread setting on your bread machine, adjusting the crust setting to medium.
4. Once done, carefully remove the bread from the machine and let it cool before slicing.

Nutritional per Serving: 190 calories, 6g protein, 36g carbohydrates, 3g fat, 2g fiber, 0mg cholesterol, 200mg sodium, 150mg potassium.

Tip: For a richer flavor, use sun-dried tomatoes packed in oil, but be sure to drain and pat them dry before chopping and adding to the dough.

44. Olive and Herb Bread

Prep time: 15 minutes | Cook time: 3 hours 40 minutes

1 ½ Pounds Loaf (≈ 12 slices):

- 1 cup + 1 tablespoon lukewarm water
- 2 tablespoons olive oil
- 3 cups bread flour
- 1 ½ teaspoons salt
- 2 tablespoons sugar
- 1 tablespoon mixed dried herbs (such as oregano, rosemary, and thyme)
- ⅓ cup chopped black olives
- 2 teaspoons active dry yeast

2 Pounds Loaf (≈ 16 slices):

- 1 ⅓ cups lukewarm water
- 3 tablespoons olive oil
- 4 cups bread flour
- 2 teaspoons salt
- 2 ½ tablespoons sugar
- 1 ½ tablespoons mixed dried herbs (such as oregano, rosemary, and thyme)
- ½ cup chopped black olives
- 2 ½ teaspoons active dry yeast

Directions:

1. Pour the water and olive oil into the bread machine pan. Then add the bread flour on top, making sure it fully covers the liquid. Sprinkle the salt, sugar, and mixed dried herbs evenly over the flour.
2. Distribute the chopped olives over the top of the flour. Make a small well in the center of the flour (without reaching the liquid) and add the yeast to this well.
3. Select the basic or white bread cycle on your bread machine, and adjust the crust to your preferred setting.
4. Once done, carefully remove the bread from the machine and let it cool before slicing.

Nutritional per Serving: 195 calories, 6g protein, 35g carbohydrates, 4g fat, 2g fiber, 0mg cholesterol, 300mg sodium, 100mg potassium.

Tip: For a more intense flavor, consider using a mix of green and black olives.

C. Nut and Seed Bread Recipes

45. Sesame Seed Bread

Prep time: 10 minutes | Cook time: 3 hours 30 minutes

1 ½ Pounds Loaf (≈ 12 slices):

- 1 cup + 2 tablespoons lukewarm water
- 2 tablespoons olive oil
- 3 cups bread flour
- 2 tablespoons sugar
- 1 teaspoon salt
- 2 tablespoons sesame seeds + for topping
- 2 teaspoons active dry yeast

2 Pounds Loaf (≈ 16 slices):

- 1 ⅓ cups lukewarm water
- 3 tablespoons olive oil
- 4 cups bread flour
- 2 ½ tablespoons sugar
- 1 ¼ teaspoons salt
- 3 tablespoons sesame seeds + for topping
- 2 ½ teaspoons active dry yeast

Directions:

1. Pour the water and olive oil into the bread machine pan. Then add the bread flour, ensuring it completely covers the liquid. Sprinkle the sugar and salt evenly over the flour.
2. Add 2 (or 3) tablespoons of sesame seeds over the top of the flour mixture. Make a small indentation in the center of the flour and add the yeast to this well.
3. Select the basic or white Bread cycle, and adjust the crust to your preferred setting.
4. After the first kneading cycle and before the second rise, brush the top of the dough with a little water or olive oil and sprinkle additional sesame seeds on top for a crunchy crust.
5. Once done, remove the bread from the machine and let it cool before slicing.

Nutritional per Serving: 180 calories, 5g protein, 35g carbohydrates, 4g fat, 2g fiber, 0mg cholesterol, 200mg sodium, 70mg potassium.

Tip: For a nuttier flavor, lightly toast the sesame seeds before adding them to the bread machine.

46. Honey Nut Bread

Prep time: 15 minutes | Cook time: 3 hours 40 minutes

1 ½ Pounds Loaf (≈ 12 slices):

- 1 cup + 2 tablespoons lukewarm water
- 2 tablespoons honey
- 2 tablespoons unsalted butter, softened
- 3 cups bread flour
- 2 tablespoons powdered milk
- 1 teaspoon salt
- 2 teaspoons active dry yeast
- ½ cup mixed nuts (walnuts, almonds), chopped

2 Pounds Loaf (≈ 16 slices):

- 1 ⅓ cups lukewarm water
- 3 tablespoons honey
- 3 tablespoons unsalted butter, softened
- 4 cups bread flour
- 2 ½ tablespoons powdered milk
- 1 ¼ teaspoons salt
- 2 ½ teaspoons active dry yeast
- ⅔ 1 cup chopped mixed nuts (e.g., walnuts, almonds).

Directions:

1. Pour the water into the bread machine pan, then add the honey and softened butter.
2. Over this, add the bread flour, ensuring to cover the liquid ingredients. Then, evenly sprinkle the powdered milk and salt over the flour.
3. Make a small indentation in the center of the flour and add the yeast to this well.
4. Select the basic or white bread cycle on your bread machine, and adjust the crust to your preferred setting.
5. Add the chopped mixed nuts about 5 minutes before the last kneading cycle ends. Once done, remove the bread from the machine and let it cool before slicing.

Nutritional per Serving: 210 calories, 6g protein, 34g carbohydrates, 5g fat, 2g fiber, 8mg cholesterol, 200mg sodium, 110mg potassium.

Tip: For a crunchier texture, lightly toast the nuts before adding them to the bread machine.

47. Almond Flaxseed Bread

Prep time: 15 minutes | Cook time: 3 hours 45 minutes

1 ½ Pounds Loaf (≈ 12 slices):

- 1 cup lukewarm water
- 2 tablespoons olive oil
- 2 cups bread flour
- 1 cup whole wheat flour
- 3 tablespoons sugar
- 1 teaspoon salt
- 2 tablespoons ground flaxseed
- ½ cup chopped almonds
- 2 teaspoons active dry yeast

2 Pounds Loaf (≈ 16 slices):

- 1 ⅓ cups lukewarm water
- 3 tablespoons olive oil
- 2 ⅔ cups bread flour
- 1 ⅓ cups whole wheat flour
- ¼ cup sugar
- 1 ¼ teaspoons salt
- 3 tablespoons ground flaxseed
- ⅔ cup chopped almonds
- 2 ½ teaspoons active dry yeast

Directions:

1. Add water and olive oil into the bread machine pan.
2. Mix together the bread flour, whole wheat flour, sugar, salt, ground flaxseed, and chopped almonds in a bowl, then add this mixture over the liquid in the bread machine pan.
3. Make a small indentation in the center of the flour mixture (but not deep enough to reach the liquid) and add the yeast to this well.
4. Select the whole wheat bread cycle on your bread machine, and adjust the crust to your preferred setting.
5. After the bread is done, carefully remove it from the machine and let it cool on a wire rack before slicing.

Nutritional per Serving: 190 calories, 6g protein, 28g carbohydrates, 7g fat, 3g fiber, 0mg cholesterol, 200mg sodium, 120mg potassium.

Tip: To enhance the nutty flavor, toast the chopped almonds before adding them to the bread mixture.

48. Walnut Rye Bread

Prep time: 15 minutes | Cook time: 3 hours 50 minutes

1 ½ Pounds Loaf (≈ 12 slices):

- 1 cup lukewarm water
- 2 tablespoons molasses
- 1 tablespoon unsalted butter, softened
- 1 ½ cups bread flour
- 1 cup rye flour
- 2 tablespoons dry milk powder
- 1 teaspoon salt
- 2 teaspoons caraway seeds
- ½ cup chopped walnuts
- 2 teaspoons active dry yeast

2 Pounds Loaf (≈ 16 slices):

- 1 ⅓ cups lukewarm water
- 3 tablespoons molasses
- 1 ½ tablespoon unsalted butter, softened
- 2 cups bread flour
- 1 ⅓ cups rye flour
- 2 ½ tablespoons dry milk powder
- 1 ¼ teaspoons salt
- 1 tablespoon caraway seeds
- ⅔ cup chopped walnuts
- 2 ½ teaspoons active dry yeast

Directions:

1. Pour water, molasses, and softened butter into the bread machine pan. Then add the bread flour and rye flour to the pan, making sure they cover the liquid ingredients. Sprinkle the dry milk powder, salt, and caraway seeds evenly over the flours.
2. Add the chopped walnuts on top of the flour mixture. Make a small well in the center of the flour and add the yeast to this well.
3. Select the whole white or basic Bread cycle, and adjust the crust to your preferred setting.
4. Once done, remove the bread from the machine and let it cool before slicing.

Nutritional per Serving: 200 calories, 6g protein, 30g carbohydrates, 7g fat, 4g fiber, 5mg cholesterol, 200mg sodium, 150mg potassium.

Tip: Toast walnuts before adding to dough for enhanced flavor and extra crunch.

Chapter 7: Cheese Breads

A. Classic Cheese Bread Recipes

49. Cheddar Cheese Bread

Prep time: 10 minutes | Cook time: 3 hours 40 minutes

1 ½ Pounds Loaf (≈ 12 slices):

- 1 cup lukewarm water
- 2 tablespoons unsalted butter, softened
- 3 cups bread flour
- 1 tablespoon sugar
- 1 ½ teaspoons salt
- 1 cup sharp cheddar cheese, grated
- 2 teaspoons active dry yeast

2 Pounds Loaf (≈ 16 slices):

- 1 ⅓ cups water
- 3 tablespoons unsalted butter, softened
- 4 cups bread flour
- 1 ½ tablespoons sugar
- 2 teaspoons salt
- 1 ⅓ cups sharp cheddar cheese, grated
- 2 ½ teaspoons active dry yeast

Directions:

1. Add the water and softened butter to the bread machine pan. Over this, evenly spread the bread flour, ensuring it covers the liquid. Sprinkle the sugar and salt over the flour.
2. Add the grated sharp cheddar cheese on top of the flour. Make a small well in the center of the flour mixture (but not deep enough to reach the liquid) and add the yeast to this well.
3. Select the basic or white bread cycle on your bread machine, and adjust the crust to your preferred setting.
4. Once done, remove the bread from the machine and let it cool before slicing.

Nutritional per Serving: 200 calories, 7g protein, 33g carbohydrates, 5g fat, 1g fiber, 20mg cholesterol, 300mg sodium, 50mg potassium.

Tip: For an extra cheesy crust, sprinkle a small amount of additional grated cheddar cheese over the top of the dough just before the final rise.

50. Parmesan Cheese Bread

Prep time: 15 minutes | Cook time: 3 hours 40 minutes

1 ½ Pounds Loaf (≈ 12 slices):

- 1 cup + 1 tablespoon lukewarm water
- 2 tablespoons olive oil
- 3 cups bread flour
- 1 tablespoon sugar
- 1 ½ teaspoons salt
- ½ cup grated Parmesan cheese
- 2 teaspoons active dry yeast

2 Pounds Loaf (≈ 16 slices):

- 1 ⅓ cups lukewarm water
- 3 tablespoons olive oil
- 4 cups bread flour
- 1 ½ tablespoons sugar
- 2 teaspoons salt
- ⅔ cup grated Parmesan cheese
- 2 ½ teaspoons active dry yeast

Directions:

1. Pour the water and olive oil into the bread machine pan.
2. Add the bread flour on top, ensuring it fully covers the liquid. Then, evenly distribute the sugar and salt over the flour.
3. Sprinkle the grated Parmesan cheese over the top of the flour mixture. Make a small indentation in the center of the flour (without reaching the liquid) and add the yeast to this well.
4. Select the basic or white bread cycle on your bread machine, and adjust the crust to your preferred setting.
5. Once done, remove the bread from the machine and let it cool before slicing.

Nutritional per Serving: 210 calories, 8g protein, 34g carbohydrates, 5g fat, 1g fiber, 10mg cholesterol, 400mg sodium, 70mg potassium.

Tip: For an enhanced Parmesan flavor and a crispy crust, sprinkle additional grated Parmesan on top of the dough just before the final rise.

51. Four Cheese Bread

Prep time: 15 minutes | Cook time: 3 hours 50 minutes

1 ½ Pounds Loaf (≈ 12 slices):

- 1 cup + 2 tablespoons lukewarm water
- 2 tablespoons olive oil
- 3 cups bread flour
- 1 tablespoon sugar and 1 ½ teaspoons salt
- ½ cup shredded mozzarella cheese
- ¼ cup grated Parmesan cheese
- ¼ cup shredded cheddar cheese
- ¼ cup crumbled feta cheese
- 2 teaspoons active dry yeast

2 Pounds Loaf (≈ 16 slices):

- 1 ⅓ cups lukewarm water
- 3 tablespoons olive oil
- 4 cups bread flour
- 1 ½ tablespoons sugar and 2 teaspoons salt
- ⅔ cup shredded mozzarella cheese
- ⅓ cup grated Parmesan cheese
- ⅓ cup shredded cheddar cheese
- ⅓ cup crumbled feta cheese
- 2 ½ teaspoons active dry yeast

Directions:

1. Pour the water and olive oil into the bread machine pan. Then, add the bread flour, ensuring it covers the liquid completely. Sprinkle the sugar and salt over the flour.
2. Distribute the mozzarella, Parmesan, cheddar, and feta cheeses evenly over the top of the flour mixture. Make a small indentation in the center of the flour (without reaching the liquid) and add the yeast to this well.
3. Select the basic or white bread cycle on your bread machine, and adjust the crust to your preferred setting.
4. Once done, remove the bread from the machine and let it cool before slicing.

Nutritional per Serving: 220 calories, 9g protein, 35g carbohydrates, 6g fat, 1g fiber, 20mg cholesterol, 450mg sodium, 80mg potassium.

Tip: For an even distribution of cheese throughout the bread, add the cheeses during the initial mixing stage to ensure they are well integrated into the dough.

52. Swiss and Bacon Bread

Prep time: 20 minutes | Cook time: 3 hours 50 minutes

1 ½ Pounds Loaf (≈ 12 slices):

- 1 cup + 1 tablespoon lukewarm water
- 2 tablespoons unsalted butter, softened
- 3 cups bread flour
- 1 tablespoon sugar
- 1 ½ teaspoons salt
- ½ cup cooked bacon, crumbled (about 8 slices)
- ½ cup Swiss cheese, grated
- 2 teaspoons active dry yeast

2 Pounds Loaf (≈ 16 slices):

- 1 ⅓ cups lukewarm water
- 3 tablespoons unsalted butter, softened
- 4 cups bread flour
- 1 ½ tablespoons sugar
- 2 teaspoons salt
- ⅔ cup cooked bacon, crumbled (about 10-12 slices)
- ⅔ cup Swiss cheese, grated
- 2 ½ teaspoons active dry yeast

Directions:

1. Pour water into the bread machine pan and add the softened butter.
2. Over this, evenly spread the bread flour, ensuring it covers the liquid. Sprinkle the sugar and salt over the flour.
3. Add the crumbled bacon and grated Swiss cheese on top of the flour mixture. Make a small indentation in the center of the flour (without reaching the liquid) and add the yeast to this well.
4. Select the basic or white bread cycle on your bread machine, and adjust the crust to your preferred setting.
5. Once done, remove the bread from the machine and let it cool before slicing.

Nutritional per Serving: 220 calories, 9g protein, 33g carbohydrates, 7g fat, 1g fiber, 20mg cholesterol, 450mg sodium, 90mg potassium.

Tip: Drain bacon well and crumble into small pieces for even distribution and optimal flavor and texture in bread.

B. Spicy Cheese Bread Recipes

53. *Pepper Jack and Jalapeño Bread*

Prep time: 20 minutes | Cook time: 3 hours 50 minutes

1 ½ Pounds Loaf (≈ 12 slices):

- 1 cup + 2 tablespoons lukewarm water
- 2 tablespoons vegetable oil
- 3 cups bread flour
- 1 tablespoon sugar and 1 ½ teaspoons salt
- 1 cup grated Pepper Jack cheese
- 2 tablespoons finely chopped jalapeño peppers (seeds removed for less heat)
- 2 teaspoons active dry yeast

2 Pounds Loaf (≈ 16 slices):

- 1 ⅓ cups lukewarm water
- 3 tablespoons vegetable oil
- 4 cups bread flour
- 1 ½ tablespoons sugar and 2 teaspoons salt
- 1 ⅓ cups grated Pepper Jack cheese
- 3 tablespoons finely chopped jalapeño peppers (seeds removed for less heat)
- 2 ½ teaspoons active dry yeast

Directions:

1. Place water and vegetable oil into the bread machine pan. After, add the bread flour on top, ensuring it fully covers the liquid. Then, sprinkle the sugar and salt evenly over the flour.
2. Distribute the grated Pepper Jack cheese and chopped jalapeño peppers over the top of the flour mixture. Make a small indentation in the center of the flour (but not deep enough to reach the liquid) and add the yeast to this well.
3. Select the basic or white bread cycle on your bread machine, and adjust the crust to your preferred setting.
4. Once done, remove the bread from the machine and let it cool before slicing.

Nutritional per Serving: 220 calories, 9g protein, 34g carbohydrates, 6g fat, 1g fiber, 20mg cholesterol, 450mg sodium, 80mg potassium.

Tip: For a milder bread, use less jalapeño or substitute with green chilies. For a hotter loaf, leave some seeds in.

54. *Cajun Spiced Gouda Bread*

Prep time: 15 minutes | Cook time: 3 hours 45 minutes

1 ½ Pounds Loaf (≈ 12 slices):

- 1 cup + 2 tablespoons lukewarm water
- 2 tablespoons unsalted butter, softened
- 3 cups bread flour
- 1 tablespoon sugar
- 1 ½ teaspoons salt
- 1 tablespoon Cajun seasoning
- ¾ cup shredded Gouda cheese
- 2 teaspoons active dry yeast

2 Pounds Loaf (≈ 16 slices):

- 1 ⅓ cups lukewarm water
- 3 tablespoons unsalted butter, softened
- 4 cups bread flour
- 1 ½ tablespoons sugar
- 2 teaspoons salt
- 1 ½ tablespoons Cajun seasoning
- 1 cup shredded Gouda cheese
- 2 ½ teaspoons active dry yeast

Directions:

1. Add the water and softened butter into the bread machine pan.
2. Over this, evenly spread the bread flour, making sure it covers the liquid. Sprinkle the sugar, salt, and Cajun seasoning over the flour.
3. Add the shredded Gouda cheese on top of the flour mixture. Make a small indentation in the center of the flour (without reaching the liquid) and add the yeast to this well.
4. Select the basic or white bread cycle on your bread machine, and adjust the crust to your preferred setting.
5. Once done, remove the bread from the machine and let it cool before slicing.

Nutritional per Serving: 225 calories, 8g protein, 34g carbohydrates, 6g fat, 1g fiber, 20mg cholesterol, 500mg sodium, 80mg potassium.

Tip: To enhance the Cajun flavor, consider adding a few dashes of hot sauce to the water before adding it to the bread machine rise.

55. Spicy Monterey Jack and Green Chile Bread

Prep time: 15 minutes | Cook time: 3 hours 50 minutes

1 ½ Pounds Loaf (≈ 12 slices):

- 1 cup + 1 tablespoon lukewarm water
- 2 tablespoons olive oil
- 3 cups bread flour
- 1 tablespoon sugar
- 1 ½ teaspoons salt
- 1 cup grated spicy Monterey Jack cheese
- ¼ cup diced green chiles (drained if using canned)
- 2 teaspoons active dry yeast

2 Pounds Loaf (≈ 16 slices):

- 1 ⅓ cups lukewarm water
- 3 tablespoons olive oil
- 4 cups bread flour
- 1 ½ tablespoons sugar
- 2 teaspoons salt
- 1 ⅓ cups grated spicy Monterey Jack cheese
- ⅓ cup diced green chiles (drained if using canned)
- 2 ½ teaspoons active dry yeast

Directions:

1. Pour water and olive oil into the bread machine pan. Then, add the bread flour, ensuring it covers the liquid. Sprinkle the sugar and salt evenly over the flour.
2. Distribute the grated spicy Monterey Jack cheese and diced green chiles over the flour. Make a small well in the center of the flour (without reaching the liquid) and add the yeast to this well.
3. Select the basic or white bread cycle on your bread machine, and adjust the crust to your preferred setting.
4. Once done, remove the bread from the machine and let it cool before slicing.

Nutritional per Serving: 230 calories, 9g protein, 35g carbohydrates, 7g fat, 1g fiber, 20mg cholesterol, 450mg sodium, 80mg potassium.

Tip: For an extra kick, add a teaspoon of chili powder to the flour mixture. This will enhance the spicy flavor of the bread.

56. Buffalo Blue Cheese Bread

Prep time: 15 minutes | Cook time: 3 hours 45 minutes

1 ½ Pounds Loaf (≈ 12 slices):

- 1 cup + 1 tablespoon lukewarm water
- 2 tablespoons unsalted butter, melted
- 3 cups bread flour
- 1 tablespoon sugar
- 1 ½ teaspoons salt
- 2 tablespoons buffalo wing sauce
- ½ cup crumbled blue cheese
- 2 teaspoons active dry yeast

2 Pounds Loaf (≈ 16 slices):

- 1 ⅓ cups lukewarm water
- 3 tablespoons unsalted butter, melted
- 4 cups bread flour
- 1 ½ tablespoons sugar
- 2 teaspoons salt
- 3 tablespoons buffalo wing sauce
- ⅔ cup crumbled blue cheese
- 2 ½ teaspoons active dry yeast

Directions:

1. Pour the water and melted butter into the bread machine pan.
2. Add the bread flour, ensuring it fully covers the liquid. Sprinkle the sugar and salt evenly over the flour.
3. Drizzle the buffalo wing sauce over the flour. Then, evenly distribute the crumbled blue cheese on top.
4. Make a small well in the center of the flour (without reaching the liquid) and add the yeast to this well.
5. Select the basic or white bread cycle on your bread machine, and adjust the crust to your preferred setting.
6. Once done, remove the bread from the machine and let it cool before slicing.

Nutritional per Serving: 210 calories, 7g protein, 34g carbohydrates, 6g fat, 1g fiber, 15mg cholesterol, 500mg sodium, 75mg potassium.

Tip: For a more intense flavor, you can add an extra tablespoon of buffalo wing sauce to the dough. Adjust according to your taste preference for spice.

C. Mediterranean Cheese Bread Recipes

57. *Feta and Olive Bread*

Prep time: 20 minutes | Cook time: 3 hours 45 minutes

1 ½ Pounds Loaf (≈ 12 slices):

- 1 cup + 2 tablespoons lukewarm water
- 2 tablespoons olive oil
- 3 cups bread flour
- 1 tablespoon sugar
- 1 ½ teaspoons salt
- ½ cup crumbled feta cheese
- ⅓ cup chopped kalamata olives
- 2 teaspoons active dry yeast

2 Pounds Loaf (≈ 16 slices):

- 1 ⅓ cups lukewarm water
- 3 tablespoons olive oil
- 4 cups bread flour
- 1 ½ tablespoons sugar
- 2 teaspoons salt
- ⅔ cup crumbled feta cheese
- ½ cup chopped kalamata olives
- 2 ½ teaspoons active dry yeast

Directions:

1. Add the water and olive oil into the bread machine pan.
2. Over this, add the bread flour, ensuring it fully covers the liquid. Sprinkle the sugar and salt evenly over the flour.
3. Distribute the crumbled feta cheese and chopped kalamata olives over the flour. Make a small well in the center of the flour (but not deep enough to reach the liquid) and add the yeast to this well.
4. Select the basic or white bread cycle on your bread machine, and adjust the crust to your preferred setting.
5. Once done, remove the bread from the machine and let it cool before slicing.

Nutritional per Serving: 210 calories, 7g protein, 34g carbohydrates, 6g fat, 2g fiber, 10mg cholesterol, 450mg sodium, 80mg potassium.

Tip: To enhance the Mediterranean flavors, consider adding a teaspoon of dried oregano or thyme to the flour mixture.

58. *Mozzarella & Basil Pesto Bread*

Prep time: 15 minutes | Cook time: 3 hours 40 minutes

1 ½ Pounds Loaf (≈ 12 slices):

- 1 cup lukewarm water
- 2 tablespoons olive oil
- 3 cups bread flour
- 2 tablespoons sugar
- 1 teaspoon salt
- ¼ cup basil pesto
- ½ cup shredded mozzarella cheese
- 2 teaspoons active dry yeast

2 Pounds Loaf (≈ 16 slices):

- 1 ⅓ cups lukewarm water
- 3 tablespoons olive oil
- 4 cups bread flour
- 2 ½ tablespoons sugar
- 1 ¼ teaspoons salt
- ⅓ cup basil pesto
- ⅔ cup shredded mozzarella cheese
- 2 ½ teaspoons active dry yeast

Directions:

1. Add the water and olive oil into the bread machine pan.
2. Over this, add the bread flour, ensuring it completely covers the liquid. Then sprinkle the sugar and salt evenly over the flour.
3. Distribute the basil pesto and shredded mozzarella cheese over the flour. Make a small well in the center of the flour (but not deep enough to reach the liquid) and add the yeast to this well.
4. Select the basic or white bread cycle on your bread machine, and adjust the crust to your preferred setting.
5. Once done, remove the bread from the machine and let it cool before slicing.

Nutritional per Serving: 220 calories, 8g protein, 34g carbohydrates, 6g fat, 1g fiber, 15mg cholesterol, 400mg sodium, 90mg potassium.

Tip: For an extra burst of flavor, consider adding a tablespoon of freshly chopped basil into the dough during the final kneading cycle.

59. Mediterranean Herb and Goat Cheese Bread

Prep time: 20 minutes | Cook time: 3 hours 50 minutes

1 ½ Pounds Loaf (≈ 12 slices):

- 1 cup + 1 tablespoon lukewarm water
- 2 tablespoons olive oil
- 3 cups bread flour
- 1 tablespoon sugar and 1 ½ teaspoons salt
- 1 tablespoon dried Mediterranean herbs (blend of oregano, basil, thyme, rosemary)
- ½ cup crumbled goat cheese
- 2 teaspoons active dry yeast

2 Pounds Loaf (≈ 16 slices):

- 1 ⅓ cups lukewarm water
- 3 tablespoons olive oil
- 4 cups bread flour
- 1 ½ tablespoons sugar and 2 teaspoons salt
- 1 ½ tablespoons dried Mediterranean herbs (blend of oregano, basil, thyme, rosemary)
- ⅔ cup crumbled goat cheese
- 2 ½ teaspoons active dry yeast

Directions:

1. Pour the water and olive oil into the bread machine pan. Then add the bread flour, ensuring it covers the liquid completely. Sprinkle the sugar and salt evenly over the flour.
2. Distribute the dried Mediterranean herbs over the flour mixture. Add the crumbled goat cheese on top of the herbs. Make a small indentation in the center of the flour (but not deep enough to reach the liquid) and add the yeast to this well.
3. Select the basic or white bread cycle on your bread machine, and adjust the crust to your preferred setting.
4. Once done, remove the bread from the machine and let it cool before slicing.

Nutritional per Serving: 215 calories, 8g protein, 34g carbohydrates, 6g fat, 1g fiber, 10mg cholesterol, 400mg sodium, 90mg potassium.

Tip: To enhance the flavor, consider adding a few sun-dried tomatoes or olives into the dough during the final kneading cycle.

60. Spinach and Feta Bread

Prep time: 20 minutes | Cook time: 3 hours 50 minutes

1 ½ Pounds Loaf (≈ 12 slices):

- 1 cup + 1 tablespoon lukewarm water
- 2 tablespoons olive oil
- 3 cups bread flour
- 1 tablespoon sugar
- 1 ½ teaspoons salt
- 1 cup fresh spinach, finely chopped
- ½ cup crumbled feta cheese
- 2 teaspoons active dry yeast

2 Pounds Loaf (≈ 16 slices):

- 1 ⅓ cups lukewarm water
- 3 tablespoons olive oil
- 4 cups bread flour
- 1 ½ tablespoons sugar
- 2 teaspoons salt
- 1 ⅓ cups fresh spinach, finely chopped
- ⅔ cup crumbled feta cheese
- 2 ½ teaspoons active dry yeast

Directions:

1. Pour the water and olive oil into the bread machine pan.
2. Add the bread flour on top, ensuring it completely covers the liquid. Sprinkle the sugar and salt evenly over the flour.
3. Distribute the finely chopped spinach and crumbled feta cheese over the flour. Make a small indentation in the center of the flour (but not deep enough to reach the liquid) and add the yeast to this well.
4. Select the basic or white bread cycle on your bread machine, and adjust the crust to your preferred setting.
5. Once done, remove the bread from the machine and let it cool before slicing.

Nutritional per Serving: 210 calories, 7g protein, 35g carbohydrates, 5g fat, 2g fiber, 15mg cholesterol, 450mg sodium, 100mg potassium.

Tip: For the best flavor and texture, ensure the spinach is thoroughly dried after washing before chopping and adding to the bread machine.

Chapter 8: Fruit Breads

A. Classic Fruit & Berry Bread Recipes

61. Classic Apple Bread

Prep time: 20 minutes | Cook time: 3 hours 40 minutes

1 ½ Pounds Loaf (≈ 12 slices):

- ¾ cup lukewarm water
- ½ cup unsweetened applesauce
- 2 tablespoons vegetable oil
- 3 cups bread flour
- 2 tablespoons sugar and 1 teaspoon salt
- 2 teaspoons active dry yeast
- ½ cup finely diced fresh apple (peeled)

2 Pounds Loaf (≈ 16 slices):

- 1 cup lukewarm water
- ⅔ cup unsweetened applesauce
- 3 tablespoons vegetable oil
- 4 cups bread flour
- 3 tablespoons sugar and 1 ¼ teaspoons salt
- 2 ½ teaspoons active dry yeast
- ⅔ cup finely diced fresh apple (peeled)

Directions:

1. In the bread machine pan, combine the water, applesauce, and vegetable oil.
2. Add the bread flour on top, ensuring it completely covers the liquid. Then, sprinkle the sugar and salt evenly over the flour.
3. Make a small indentation in the center of the flour and add the yeast to this well.
4. Select the sweet, basic or white bread cycle on your bread machine, and adjust the crust to your preferred setting.
5. At the fruit/nut signal or 5 minutes before the last kneading cycle ends, add the finely diced apple.
6. Once done, remove the bread from the machine and let it cool before slicing.

Nutritional per Serving: 180 calories, 5g protein, 35g carbohydrates, 2g fat, 1g fiber, 0mg cholesterol, 200mg sodium, 50mg potassium.

Tip: To bring out more of the apple flavor, consider adding a teaspoon of cinnamon to the dough mixture.

62. Classic Fruit and Nut Bread

Prep time: 20 minutes | Cook time: 3 hours 45 minutes

1 ½ Pounds Loaf (≈ 12 slices):

- ¾ cup lukewarm water
- 2 tablespoons vegetable oil
- 3 cups bread flour
- 2 tablespoons sugar and 1 teaspoon salt
- 2 teaspoons active dry yeast
- ½ cup mixed dried fruit (raisins, cranberries, chopped apricots)
- ½ cup mixed nuts (walnuts, almonds, chopped)

2 Pounds Loaf (≈ 16 slices):

- 1 cup water
- 3 tablespoons vegetable oil
- 4 cups bread flour
- 3 tablespoons sugar and 1 ¼ teaspoons salt
- 2 ½ teaspoons active dry yeast
- ⅔ cup mixed dried fruit (raisins, cranberries, chopped apricots)
- ⅔ cup mixed nuts (walnuts, almonds, chopped)

Directions:

1. Pour the water and vegetable oil into the bread machine pan. Then, add the bread flour on top, making sure it fully covers the liquid. Then, evenly distribute the sugar and salt over the flour.
2. Make a small indentation in the center of the flour and add the yeast to this well.
3. Select the sweet, basic or white Bread cycle, and adjust the crust to your preferred setting.
4. At the machine's fruit and nut signal or 5 minutes before the last kneading cycle ends, add the mixed dried fruit and nuts.
5. Once done, remove the bread from the machine and let it cool before slicing.

Nutritional per Serving: 210 calories, 6g protein, 37g carbohydrates, 5g fat, 2g fiber, 0mg cholesterol, 200mg sodium, 100mg potassium.

Tip: For the best results, chop the nuts and fruit into small pieces to ensure they are evenly distributed throughout the bread.

63. Classic Banana Berry Bread

Prep time: 20 minutes | Cook time: 3 hours 40 minutes

1 ½ Pounds Loaf (≈ 12 slices):

- ¾ cup mashed ripe banana (≈ 1 ½ bananas)
- ½ cup lukewarm water
- 2 tablespoons vegetable oil
- 3 cups bread flour
- 2 tablespoons sugar and 1 teaspoon salt
- 2 teaspoons active dry yeast
- ½ cup mixed berries (fresh or frozen - such as raspberries, blueberries, and chopped strawberries)

2 Pounds Loaf (≈ 16 slices):

- 1 cup mashed ripe banana (≈ 2 bananas)
- ⅔ cup lukewarm water
- 3 tablespoons vegetable oil
- 4 cups bread flour
- 3 tablespoons sugar and 1 ¼ teaspoons salt
- 2 ½ teaspoons active dry yeast
- ⅔ cup mixed berries (fresh or frozen - such as raspberries, blueberries, and chopped strawberries)

Directions:

1. In the bread machine pan, combine the mashed banana, water, and vegetable oil.
2. Over this, add the bread flour, making sure it completely covers the liquid. Then, evenly sprinkle the sugar and salt over the flour.
3. Make a small indentation in the center of the flour (but not deep enough to reach the liquid) and add the yeast to this well.
4. Select the sweet, basic or white Bread cycle, and adjust the crust to your preferred setting.
5. At the fruit/nut signal or 5 minutes before the last kneading cycle ends, gently add the mixed berries.
6. Once done, remove the bread from the machine and let it cool before slicing.

Nutritional per Serving: 190 calories, 5g protein, 37g carbohydrates, 3g fat, 2g fiber, 0mg cholesterol, 200mg sodium, 80mg potassium.

Tip: If using frozen berries, do not thaw them before adding to the dough; this helps prevent the berries from bleeding too much color into the bread.

64. Pear and Cranberry Bread

Prep time: 20 minutes | Cook time: 3 hours 45 minutes

1 ½ Pounds Loaf (≈ 12 slices):

- ¾ cup lukewarm water
- ½ cup pear puree (from about 1 medium ripe pear)
- 2 tablespoons vegetable oil
- 3 cups bread flour
- 2 tablespoons sugar
- 1 teaspoon salt
- 2 teaspoons active dry yeast
- ½ cup dried cranberries

2 Pounds Loaf (≈ 16 slices):

- 1 cup lukewarm water
- ⅔ cup pear puree (from about 1 large ripe pear)
- 3 tablespoons vegetable oil
- 4 cups bread flour
- 3 tablespoons sugar
- 1 ¼ teaspoons salt
- 2 ½ teaspoons active dry yeast
- ⅔ cup dried cranberries

Directions:

1. In the bread machine pan, mix the water, pear puree, and vegetable oil.
2. Add the bread flour on top, ensuring it completely covers the liquid mixture. Then, sprinkle the sugar and salt evenly over the flour.
3. Make a small indentation in the center of the flour and add the yeast to this well.
4. Select the sweet, basic or white Bread cycle, and adjust the crust to your preferred setting.
5. At the fruit/nut signal or 5 minutes before the last kneading cycle ends, add the dried cranberries.
6. Once done, remove the bread from the machine and let it cool before slicing.

Nutritional per Serving: 90 calories, 5g protein, 38g carbohydrates, 3g fat, 2g fiber, 0mg cholesterol, 200mg sodium, 90mg potassium.

Tip: For an added touch of sweetness and texture, sprinkle cinnamon and sugar on cranberries before mixing into dough.

B. Citrus-Inspired Bread Recipes

65. *Lemon Poppy Seed Bread*

Prep time: 15 minutes | Cook time: 3 hours 40 minutes

1 ½ Pounds Loaf (≈ 12 slices):

- 1 cup + 1 tablespoon lukewarm water
- 2 tablespoons vegetable oil
- 3 cups bread flour
- 2 tablespoons sugar
- 1 teaspoon salt
- 2 tablespoons poppy seeds
- 2 teaspoons grated lemon zest
- 2 teaspoons active dry yeast

2 Pounds Loaf (≈ 16 slices):

- 1 ⅓ cups lukewarm water
- 3 tablespoons vegetable oil
- 4 cups bread flour
- 3 tablespoons sugar
- 1 ¼ teaspoons salt
- 3 tablespoons poppy seeds
- 1 tablespoon grated lemon zest
- 2 ½ teaspoons active dry yeast

Directions:

1. Pour the water and vegetable oil into the bread machine pan.
2. Add the bread flour on top, ensuring it completely covers the liquid. Then, evenly distribute the sugar, salt, poppy seeds, and grated lemon zest over the flour.
3. Make a small indentation in the center of the flour mixture (but not deep enough to reach the liquid) and add the yeast to this well.
4. Select the sweet, basic or white bread cycle on your bread machine, adjust the crust to your preferred setting.
5. Once done, remove the bread from the machine and let it cool before slicing.

Nutritional per Serving: 190 calories, 6g protein, 35g carbohydrates, 4g fat, 2g fiber, 0mg cholesterol, 200mg sodium, 70mg potassium.

Tip: For a more pronounced lemon flavor, consider adding a tablespoon of fresh lemon juice to the water before adding it to the bread machine.

66. *Grapefruit Almond Bread*

Prep time: 20 minutes | Cook time: 3 hours 45 minutes

1 ½ Pounds Loaf (≈ 12 slices):

- ¾ cup grapefruit juice (freshly squeezed preferred)
- ¼ cup lukewarm water
- 2 tablespoons vegetable oil
- 3 cups bread flour
- 2 tablespoons sugar and 1 teaspoon salt
- 2 teaspoons grated grapefruit zest
- ½ cup chopped almonds
- 2 teaspoons active dry yeast

2 Pounds Loaf (≈ 16 slices):

- 1 cup grapefruit juice (freshly squeezed preferred)
- ⅓ cup lukewarm water
- 3 tablespoons vegetable oil
- 4 cups bread flour
- 3 tablespoons sugar and 1 ¼ teaspoons salt
- 1 tablespoon grated grapefruit zest
- ⅔ cup chopped almonds
- 2 ½ teaspoons active dry yeast

Directions:

1. Combine the grapefruit juice, water, and vegetable oil in the bread machine pan.
2. Add the bread flour on top, ensuring it fully covers the liquid. Sprinkle the sugar, salt, and grated grapefruit zest over the flour.
3. Distribute the chopped almonds over the flour mixture. Make a small indentation in the center of the flour (without reaching the liquid) and add the yeast to this well.
4. Select the sweet, basic or white bread cycle on your bread machine, adjust the crust to your preferred setting.
5. Once done, remove the bread from the machine and let it cool before slicing.

Nutritional per Serving: 200 calories, 6g protein, 36g carbohydrates, 5g fat, 2g fiber, 0mg cholesterol, 200mg sodium, 80mg potassium.

Tip: To intensify the grapefruit flavor, consider adding an extra tablespoon of grapefruit zest to the dough mixture.

67. Orange Chocolate Chip Bread

Prep time: 20 minutes | Cook time: 3 hours 45 minutes

1 ½ Pounds Loaf (≈ 12 slices):

- ¾ cup + 2 tablespoons orange juice (freshly squeezed preferred)
- 2 tablespoons unsalted butter, melted
- 3 cups bread flour
- 2 tablespoons sugar
- 1 teaspoon salt
- 2 teaspoons grated orange zest
- ½ cup semisweet chocolate chips
- 2 teaspoons active dry yeast

2 Pounds Loaf (≈ 16 slices):

- cup + 1 tablespoon orange juice (freshly squeezed preferred)
- 3 tablespoons unsalted butter, melted
- 4 cups bread flour
- 3 tablespoons sugar
- 1 ¼ teaspoons salt
- 1 tablespoon grated orange zest
- ⅔ cup semisweet chocolate chips
- 2 ½ teaspoons active dry yeast

Directions:

1. Pour the orange juice and melted butter into the bread machine pan.
2. Add the bread flour, ensuring it completely covers the liquid. Then, sprinkle the sugar, salt, and grated orange zest over the flour.
3. Make a small indentation in the center of the flour mixture (but not deep enough to reach the liquid) and add the yeast to this well.
4. Select the sweet, basic or white Bread cycle, and adjust the crust to your preferred setting.
5. At the machine's add-in signal, or 5 minutes before the last kneading cycle ends, add the semisweet chocolate chips.
6. Once done, remove the bread from the machine and let it cool before slicing.

Nutritional per Serving: 210 calories, 5g protein, 37g carbohydrates, 6g fat, 2g fiber, 10mg cholesterol, 200mg sodium, 100mg potassium.

Tip: For a richer orange flavor, you can add a few drops of orange extract along with the orange zest.

68. Lemon Blueberry Bread

Prep time: 20 minutes | Cook time: 3 hours 50 minutes

1 ½ Pounds Loaf (≈ 12 slices):

- ¾ cup + 2 tablespoons lukewarm water
- 2 tablespoons unsalted butter, melted
- 3 cups bread flour
- 2 tablespoons sugar
- 1 teaspoon salt
- 2 teaspoons grated lemon zest
- ½ cup fresh or frozen blueberries
- 2 teaspoons active dry yeast

2 Pounds Loaf (≈ 16 slices):

- 1 cup + 1 tablespoon lukewarm water
- 3 tablespoons unsalted butter, melted
- 4 cups bread flour
- 3 tablespoons sugar
- 1 ¼ teaspoons salt
- 1 tablespoon grated lemon zest
- ⅔ cup fresh or frozen blueberries
- 2 ½ teaspoons active dry yeast

Directions:

1. Pour the water and melted butter into the bread machine pan.
2. Add the bread flour, ensuring it covers the liquid. Sprinkle the sugar, salt, and grated lemon zest over the flour.
3. Make a small well in the center of the flour mixture (but not deep enough to reach the liquid) and add the yeast to this well.
4. Select the sweet, basic or white bread cycle on your bread machine, adjust the crust to your preferred setting.
5. At the machine's add-in signal, or 5 minutes before the last kneading cycle ends, carefully add the blueberries.
6. Once the bread cycle is complete, carefully remove the bread from the pan and let it cool on a wire rack before slicing.

Nutritional per Serving: 190 calories, 5g protein, 36g carbohydrates, 3g fat, 1g fiber, 8mg cholesterol, 200mg sodium, 50mg potassium.

Tip: If using frozen blueberries, do not thaw them before adding to the dough to prevent the bread from turning blue.

C. Exotic Fruit Bread Recipes

69. *Coconut Bread*

Prep time: 15 minutes | Cook time: 3 hours 40 minutes

1 ½ Pounds Loaf (≈ 12 slices):

- 1 cup coconut milk
- 2 tablespoons vegetable oil
- 3 cups bread flour
- 2 tablespoons sugar
- 1 teaspoon salt
- ½ cup shredded coconut
- 2 teaspoons active dry yeast

2 Pounds Loaf (≈ 16 slices):

- 1 ⅓ cups coconut milk
- 3 tablespoons vegetable oil
- 4 cups bread flour
- 3 tablespoons sugar
- 1 ¼ teaspoons salt
- ⅔ cup shredded coconut
- 2 ½ teaspoons active dry yeast

Directions:

1. Pour the coconut milk and vegetable oil into the bread machine pan.
2. Add the bread flour, ensuring it completely covers the liquid. Sprinkle the sugar and salt evenly over the flour.
3. Distribute the shredded coconut over the flour. Make a small well in the center of the flour (but not deep enough to reach the liquid) and add the yeast to this well.
4. Select the sweet, basic or white bread cycle on your bread machine, adjust the crust to your preferred setting.
5. Once the bread cycle is complete, carefully remove the bread from the machine and let it cool on a wire rack before slicing.

Nutritional per Serving: 210 calories, 5g protein, 34g carbohydrates, 6g fat, 2g fiber, 0mg cholesterol, 200mg sodium, 80mg potassium.

Tip: Toasting the shredded coconut before adding it to the bread machine can enhance its flavor and texture in the final bread.

70. *Kiwi Lime Bread*

Prep time: 20 minutes | Cook time: 3 hours 45 minutes

1 ½ Pounds Loaf (≈ 12 slices):

- ¾ cup lukewarm water
- ¼ cup lime juice
- 2 tablespoons vegetable oil
- 3 cups bread flour
- 2 tablespoons sugar1 teaspoon salt
- 2 teaspoons grated lime zest
- ½ cup finely chopped kiwi
- 2 teaspoons active dry yeast

2 Pounds Loaf (≈ 16 slices):

- 1 cup lukewarm water
- ⅓ cup lime juice
- 3 tablespoons vegetable oil
- 4 cups bread flour
- 3 tablespoons sugar and 1 ¼ teaspoons salt
- 1 tablespoon grated lime zest
- ⅔ cup finely chopped kiwi
- 2 ½ teaspoons active dry yeast

Directions:

1. In the bread machine pan, mix the water, lime juice, and vegetable oil.
2. Add the bread flour on top, making sure it completely covers the liquid mixture. Then, sprinkle the sugar, salt, and grated lime zest over the flour.
3. Distribute the finely chopped kiwi evenly over the flour. Make a small well in the center of the flour and add the yeast to this well.
4. Select the sweet, basic or white bread cycle on your bread machine, adjust the crust to your preferred setting.
5. Once done, remove the bread from the machine and let it cool before slicing.

Nutritional per Serving: 190 calories, 5g protein, 36g carbohydrates, 3g fat, 1g fiber, 0mg cholesterol, 200mg sodium, 90mg potassium.

Tip: To ensure the kiwi doesn't overly moisten the dough, you might lightly coat the chopped kiwi in a bit of flour before adding it to the bread machine. It helps to absorb excess moisture and distribute the fruit evenly throughout the bread.

71. Pineapple Banana Bread

Prep time: 20 minutes | Cook time: 3 hours 45 minutes

1 ½ Pounds Loaf (≈ 12 slices):

- ½ cup mashed ripe banana (≈ 1 banana)
- ½ cup crushed pineapple, drained
- ¼ cup pineapple juice (use juice drained from crushed pineapple)
- 2 tablespoons vegetable oil
- 3 cups bread flour
- 2 tablespoons sugar
- 1 teaspoon salt
- 2 teaspoons active dry yeast

2 Pounds Loaf (≈ 16 slices):

- ⅔ cup mashed ripe banana (≈ 1 ½ banana)
- ⅔ cup crushed pineapple, drained
- ⅓ cup pineapple juice (use juice drained from crushed pineapple)
- 3 tablespoons vegetable oil
- 4 cups bread flour
- 3 tablespoons sugar
- 1 ¼ teaspoons salt
- 2 ½ teaspoons active dry yeast

Directions:

1. In the bread machine pan, combine the mashed banana, crushed pineapple, pineapple juice, and vegetable oil.
2. Add the bread flour on top, making sure it fully covers the liquid mixture. Then, sprinkle the sugar and salt evenly over the flour.
3. Make a small indentation in the center of the flour (but not deep enough to reach the liquid) and add the yeast to this well.
4. Select the basic or white bread cycle on your bread machine, adjusting the crust setting to medium.
5. Once the bread cycle is complete, carefully remove the bread from the machine and allow it to cool on a wire rack before slicing.

Nutritional per Serving: 190 calories, 5g protein, 37g carbohydrates, 3g fat, 1g fiber, 0mg cholesterol, 200mg sodium, 80mg potassium.

Tip: For an extra touch of flavor, you can add a teaspoon of vanilla extract or a sprinkle of cinnamon to the dough mixture.

72. Avocado Bread

Prep time: 20 minutes | Cook time: 3 hours 45 minutes

1 ½ Pounds Loaf (≈ 12 slices):

- ¾ cup mashed ripe avocado (≈ 1 medium avocado)
- ½ cup lukewarm water
- 2 tablespoons olive oil
- 3 cups bread flour
- 2 tablespoons sugar
- 1 teaspoon salt
- 2 teaspoons active dry yeast

2 Pounds Loaf (≈ 16 slices):

- 1 cup mashed ripe avocado (≈ 1 large avocado)
- ⅔ cup lukewarm water
- 3 tablespoons olive oil
- 4 cups bread flour
- 3 tablespoons sugar
- 1 ¼ teaspoons salt
- 2 ½ teaspoons active dry yeast

Directions:

1. In the bread machine pan, combine the mashed avocado, water, and olive oil.
2. Add the bread flour on top, ensuring it fully covers the liquid mixture. Then, sprinkle the sugar and salt evenly over the flour.
3. Make a small indentation in the center of the flour (but not deep enough to reach the liquid) and add the yeast to this well.
4. Select the basic or white bread cycle on your bread machine, adjusting the crust setting to medium.
5. Once the bread cycle is complete, carefully remove the bread from the machine and let it cool on a wire rack before slicing.

Nutritional per Serving: 200 calories, 6g protein, 35g carbohydrates, 4g fat, 2g fiber, 0mg cholesterol, 200mg sodium, 100mg potassium.

Tip: To enhance the avocado flavor and add a nutritional boost, consider adding a tablespoon of chia seeds or flaxseeds to the dough mixture.

Chapter 9: Diet Breads

A. Vegan Bread Recipes

73. *Basic Vegan White Bread*

Prep time: 10 minutes | Cook time: 3 hours 30 minutes

1 ½ Pounds Loaf (≈ 12 slices):

- 1 cup + 2 tablespoons lukewarm water
- 2 tablespoons olive oil
- 3 cups bread flour
- 2 tablespoons sugar
- 1 ½ teaspoons salt
- 2 teaspoons active dry yeast

2 Pounds Loaf (≈ 16 slices):

- 1 ⅓ cups water
- 3 tablespoons olive oil
- 4 cups bread flour
- 3 tablespoons sugar
- 2 teaspoons salt
- 2 ½ teaspoons active dry yeast

Directions:

1. Add the water and olive oil to the bread machine pan.
2. Over this, add the bread flour, ensuring it fully covers the liquid. Then, evenly distribute the sugar and salt over the flour.
3. Make a small well in the center of the flour (but not deep enough to reach the liquid) and add the yeast to this well.
4. Select the basic or white bread cycle on your bread machine, adjusting the crust setting to medium.
5. Once the bread cycle is complete, carefully remove the bread from the pan and let it cool on a wire rack before slicing.

Nutritional per Serving: 180 calories, 5g protein, 34g carbohydrates, 3g fat, 1g fiber, 0mg cholesterol, 300mg sodium, 50mg potassium.

Tip: For a healthier twist, substitute 1 cup of the bread flour with whole wheat flour to add more fiber and nutrients to your bread.

74. *Whole Wheat Vegan Bread*

Prep time: 15 minutes | Cook time: 3 hours 50 minutes

1 ½ Pounds Loaf (≈ 12 slices):

- 1 ¼ cups lukewarm water
- 2 tablespoons maple syrup
- 2 tablespoons olive oil
- 2 cups whole wheat flour
- 1 cup bread flour
- 1 ½ teaspoons salt
- 2 teaspoons active dry yeast

2 Pounds Loaf (≈ 16 slices):

- 1 ½ cups lukewarm water
- 3 tablespoons maple syrup
- 3 tablespoons olive oil
- 2 ⅔ cups whole wheat flour
- 1 ⅓ cups bread flour
- 2 teaspoons salt
- 2 ½ teaspoons active dry yeast

Directions:

1. Pour the water, maple syrup, and olive oil into the bread machine pan.
2. Add both the whole wheat flour and bread flour, making sure they fully cover the liquid. Sprinkle the salt evenly over the flours.
3. Make a small indentation in the center of the flour mixture (but not deep enough to reach the liquid) and add the yeast to this well.
4. Select the whole wheat bread cycle on your bread machine, adjusting the crust setting to medium.
5. Once the bread cycle is complete, carefully remove the bread from the pan and let it cool on a wire rack before slicing.

Nutritional per Serving: 190 calories, 6g protein, 36g carbohydrates, 4g fat, 4g fiber, 0mg cholesterol, 300mg sodium, 100mg potassium.

Tip: For added texture and nutrition, consider mixing in a tablespoon of flaxseeds or sunflower seeds during the final kneading cycle.

75. Vegan Herb Bread

Prep time: 15 minutes | Cook time: 3 hours 40 minutes

1 ½ Pounds Loaf (≈ 12 slices):

- 1 cup + 2 tablespoons lukewarm water
- 2 tablespoons olive oil
- 3 cups bread flour
- 2 tablespoons sugar
- 1 ½ teaspoons salt
- 1 tablespoon dried Italian herbs (basil, oregano, thyme)
- 2 teaspoons active dry yeast

2 Pounds Loaf (≈ 16 slices):

- 1 ⅓ cups lukewarm water
- 3 tablespoons olive oil
- 4 cups bread flour
- 3 tablespoons sugar
- 2 teaspoons salt
- 1 ½ tablespoons dried Italian herbs (basil, oregano, thyme)
- 2 ½ teaspoons active dry yeast

Directions:

1. Pour the water and olive oil into the bread machine pan.
2. Add the bread flour on top, ensuring it fully covers the liquid. Then, evenly distribute the sugar, salt, and dried Italian herbs over the flour.
3. Make a small indentation in the center of the flour mixture (but not deep enough to reach the liquid) and add the yeast to this well.
4. Select the basic or white bread cycle on your bread machine, adjusting the crust setting to medium.
5. Once the bread cycle is complete, carefully remove the bread from the machine and let it cool on a wire rack before slicing.

Nutritional per Serving: 80 calories, 5g protein, 35g carbohydrates, 3g fat, 1g fiber, 0mg cholesterol, 300mg sodium, 80mg potassium.

Tip: For a fresher herb flavor, you can add a tablespoon of freshly chopped herbs to the dough during the final kneading cycle.

76. Vegan Rye Bread

Prep time: 15 minutes | Cook time: 3 hours 50 minutes

1 ½ Pounds Loaf (≈ 12 slices):

- 1 cup lukewarm water
- ¼ cup apple cider vinegar (to mimic the tanginess of traditional rye bread)
- 2 tablespoons molasses (for color and slight sweetness)
- 1 ½ cups bread flour
- 1 ½ cups rye flour
- 2 tablespoons cocoa powder (for color)
- 1 tablespoon sugar and 1 ½ teaspoons salt
- 2 teaspoons caraway seeds (optional)
- 2 teaspoons active dry yeast

2 Pounds Loaf (≈ 16 slices):

- 1 ⅓ cups lukewarm water
- ⅓ cup apple cider vinegar
- 3 tablespoons molasses
- 2 cups bread flour
- 2 cups rye flour
- 2 ½ tablespoons cocoa powder
- 1 ½ tablespoons sugar and 2 teaspoons salt
- 1 tablespoon caraway seeds (optional)
- 2 ½ teaspoons active dry yeast

Directions:

1. In the bread machine pan, combine the water, apple cider vinegar, and molasses.
2. Add both the bread flour and rye flour, ensuring they fully cover the liquid. Then, sprinkle the cocoa powder, sugar, salt, and caraway seeds (if using) evenly over the flours.
3. Make a small indentation in the center of the flour mixture and add the yeast to this well.
4. Select the whole wheat or basic Bread cycle, and adjust the crust to your preferred setting.
5. Once done, remove the bread from the machine and let it cool before slicing.

Nutritional per Serving: 160 calories, 4g protein, 34g carbohydrates, 1g fat, 3g fiber, 0mg cholesterol, 300mg sodium, 150mg potassium.

Tip: Add a tablespoon of coffee or espresso powder with cocoa powder to deepen flavors without a coffee taste, enhancing rye and cocoa.

77. Vegan Oatmeal Bread

Prep time: 15 minutes | Cook time: 3 hours 30 minutes

1 ½ Pounds Loaf (≈ 12 slices):

- 1 cup lukewarm water
- ¼ cup maple syrup or agave nectar
- 2 tablespoons vegetable oil
- 2 cups bread flour
- 1 cup rolled oats
- 1 teaspoon salt
- 2 teaspoons active dry yeast

2 Pounds Loaf (≈ 16 slices):

- 1 ⅓ cups lukewarm water
- ⅓ cup maple syrup or agave nectar
- 3 tablespoons vegetable oil
- 2 ⅔ cups bread flour
- 1 ⅓ cups rolled oats
- 1 ¼ teaspoons salt
- 2 ½ teaspoons active dry yeast

Directions:

1. Pour the water, maple syrup (or agave nectar), and vegetable oil into the bread machine pan.
2. Add the bread flour and rolled oats, ensuring they fully cover the liquid mixture. Then, sprinkle the salt evenly over the flour and oats.
3. Make a small indentation in the center of the flour and oats (but not deep enough to reach the liquid) and add the yeast to this well.
4. Select the basic or whole wheat bread cycle on your bread machine, adjust the crust to your preferred setting.
5. Once the bread cycle is complete, carefully remove the bread from the machine and let it cool on a wire rack before slicing.

Nutritional per Serving: 190 calories, 5g protein, 37g carbohydrates, 3g fat, 2g fiber, 0mg cholesterol, 200mg sodium, 90mg potassium.

Tip: For added texture and nutrition, consider stirring in a quarter cup of your favorite seeds (such as flaxseed, sunflower seeds, or pumpkin seeds) into the dough at the add-in signal.

78. Vegan Walnut Raisin Bread

Prep time: 20 minutes | Cook time: 3 hours 40 minutes

1 ½ Pounds Loaf (≈ 12 slices):

- 1 cup + 2 tablespoons lukewarm water
- 2 tablespoons maple syrup
- 2 tablespoons vegetable oil
- 3 cups bread flour
- 1 teaspoon salt
- 2 teaspoons cinnamon
- 2 teaspoons active dry yeast
- ½ cup raisins
- ½ cup chopped walnuts

2 Pounds Loaf (≈ 16 slices):

- 1 ⅓ cups lukewarm water
- 3 tablespoons maple syrup
- 3 tablespoons vegetable oil
- 4 cups bread flour
- 1 ¼ teaspoons salt
- 1 tablespoon cinnamon
- 2 ½ teaspoons active dry yeast
- ⅔ cup raisins
- ⅔ cup chopped walnuts

Directions:

1. Pour the water, maple syrup, and vegetable oil into the bread machine pan.
2. Add the bread flour on top, ensuring it fully covers the liquid mixture. Sprinkle the salt and cinnamon evenly over the flour.
3. Make a small well in the center of the flour mixture and add the yeast to this well.
4. Select the whole wheat or basic Bread cycle, and adjust the crust to your preferred setting.
5. At the machine's add-in signal, or 5 minutes before the last kneading cycle ends, add the raisins and chopped walnuts.
6. Once done, remove the bread from the machine and let it cool before slicing.

Nutritional per Serving: 220 calories, 6g protein, 39g carbohydrates, 5g fat, 2g fiber, 0mg cholesterol, 200mg sodium, 120mg potassium.

Tip: Toss raisins and walnuts with flour before adding to the bread machine for even distribution and to prevent sinking.

B. Gluten-Free Bread Recipes

79. *Gluten-Free Sandwich Bread*

Prep time: 15 minutes | Cook time: 2 hours 50 minutes

1 ½ Pounds Loaf (≈ 12 slices):

- 1 cup warm water (about 110°F)
- 3 tablespoons olive oil
- 2 eggs (room temperature, lightly beaten)
- 1 teaspoon apple cider vinegar
- 2 cups gluten-free flour blend (ensure it includes xanthan gum if not already included in the mix)
- 1 tablespoon sugar and 1 ½ teaspoons salt
- 2 teaspoons active dry yeast

2 Pounds Loaf (≈ 16 slices):

- 1 ⅓ cups warm water (about 110°F)
- ¼ cup olive oil
- 3 eggs (room temperature, lightly beaten)
- 1 ½ teaspoons apple cider vinegar
- 2 ⅔ cups gluten-free flour blend (ensure it includes xanthan gum if not already included in the mix)
- 1 ½ tablespoons sugar
- 2 teaspoons salt
- 2 ½ teaspoons active dry yeast

Directions:

1. In a bowl, whisk together the warm water, olive oil, eggs, and apple cider vinegar.
2. Add the liquid mixture to the bread machine pan. Over this, add the gluten-free flour blend. Then, evenly distribute the sugar and salt over the flour.
3. Make a small well in the center of the flour and add the yeast to this well.
4. Select the gluten-free or basic Bread cycle, and adjust the crust to your preferred setting.
5. Once done, remove the bread from the machine and let it cool before slicing.

Nutritional per Serving: 180 calories, 4g protein, 28g carbohydrates, 7g fat, 2g fiber, 35mg cholesterol, 300mg sodium, 50mg potassium.

Tip: For a softer crust, brush the top of the bread with a little olive oil or melted butter immediately after baking. This will add moisture to the crust, making it softer and more palatable.

80. *Gluten-Free Cinnamon Raisin Bread*

Prep time: 20 minutes | Cook time: 3 hours 40 minutes

1 ½ Pounds Loaf (≈ 12 slices):

- 1 cup warm water (about 110°F)
- 3 tablespoons vegetable oil
- 2 eggs (room temperature, lightly beaten)
- 1 teaspoon apple cider vinegar
- 2 ½ cups gluten-free flour blend
- ¼ cup sugar and 1 teaspoon salt
- 1 tablespoon ground cinnamon
- 2 teaspoons active dry yeast
- ½ cup raisins

2 Pounds Loaf (≈ 16 slices):

- 1 ⅓ cups warm water (about 110°F)
- ¼ cup vegetable oil
- 3 eggs (room temperature, lightly beaten)
- 1 ½ teaspoons apple cider vinegar
- 3 ⅓ cups gluten-free flour blend
- ⅓ cup sugar and 1 ¼ teaspoons salt
- 1 ½ tablespoons ground cinnamon
- 2 ½ teaspoons active dry yeast
- ⅔ cup raisins

Directions:

1. In a bowl, combine the warm water, vegetable oil, eggs, and apple cider vinegar. Pour this liquid mixture into the bread machine pan. After, add the gluten-free flour blend over the liquid. Then, sprinkle the sugar, salt, and ground cinnamon evenly over the flour.
2. Make a small well in the center of the flour mixture and add the yeast to this well.
3. Select the gluten-free or basic Bread cycle, and adjust the crust to your preferred setting.
4. Add the raisins, about 5 minutes before the last kneading cycle ends.
5. Once done, remove the bread from the machine and let it cool before slicing.

Nutritional per Serving: 200 calories, 4g protein, 38g carbohydrates, 5g fat, 2g fiber, 30mg cholesterol, 200mg sodium, 80mg potassium.

Tip: Soak raisins in warm water for 10 minutes before adding to the machine for plumper, more flavorful results.

81. Gluten-Free Sunflower Seed Bread

Prep time: 20 minutes | Cook time: 3 hours 50 minutes

1 ½ Pounds Loaf (≈ 12 slices):

- 1 cup warm water (about 110°F)
- 3 tablespoons honey
- 2 tablespoons vegetable oil
- 3 cups gluten-free all-purpose flour blend
- 1 tablespoon ground flaxseed (optional)
- 1 teaspoon salt
- 2 teaspoons xanthan gum (if not included in your flour blend)
- 2 teaspoons active dry yeast
- ½ cup raw sunflower seeds and topping

2 Pounds Loaf (≈ 16 slices):

- 1 ⅓ cups warm water (about 110°F)
- ¼ cup honey
- 3 tablespoons vegetable oil
- 4 cups gluten-free all-purpose flour blend
- 1 ½ tablespoons ground flaxseed (optional)
- 1 ¼ teaspoons salt
- 2 ½ teaspoons xanthan gum (if not included in your flour blend)
- 2 ½ teaspoons active dry yeast
- ⅔ cup raw sunflower seeds and topping

Directions:

1. Combine the warm water, honey and vegetable oil in the bread machine pan.
2. Add the gluten-free flour blend, ground flaxseed (if using), salt, and xanthan gum over the liquid. Ensure the dry ingredients fully cover the liquid.
3. Make a small indentation in the center of the dry ingredients and add the yeast to this well.
4. Select the gluten-free or basic Bread cycle, and adjust the crust to your preferred setting.
5. Add the sunflower seeds about 5 minutes before the last kneading cycle ends.
6. Once done, remove the bread from the machine and let it cool before slicing.

Nutritional per Serving: 210 calories, 5g protein, 35g carbohydrates, 6g fat, 3g fiber, 0mg cholesterol, 200mg sodium, 90mg potassium.

Tip: Lightly toast sunflower seeds before adding to the machine for a nuttier flavor and extra crunch.

82. Gluten-Free Raisin Bread

Prep time: 20 minutes | Cook time: 3 hours 30 minutes

1 ½ Pounds Loaf (≈ 12 slices):

- 1 cup warm water (about 110°F)
- 2 tablespoons vegetable oil
- 2 eggs, beaten
- 1 teaspoon apple cider vinegar
- 2 ½ cups gluten-free all-purpose flour blend
- ¼ cup sugar and 1 teaspoon salt
- 1 teaspoon cinnamon
- 1 tablespoon xanthan gum (if not included in your flour blend)
- 2 teaspoons active dry yeast
- ½ cup raisins

2 Pounds Loaf (≈ 16 slices):

- ⅓ cups warm water (about 110°F)
- 3 tablespoons vegetable oil
- 3 eggs, beaten
- 1 ½ teaspoons apple cider vinegar
- 3 ⅓ cups gluten-free all-purpose flour blend
- ⅓ cup sugar and 1 ¼ teaspoons salt
- 1 ½ teaspoons cinnamon
- 1 ½ tablespoons xanthan gum
- 2 ½ teaspoons active dry yeast
- ⅔ cup raisins

Directions:

1. Combine warm water, vegetable oil, beaten eggs, and apple cider vinegar in the bread machine pan. Add gluten-free flour blend on top, then evenly sprinkle sugar, cinnamon, salt, and xanthan gum over it.
2. Make a small well in the center of the flour mixture and add the yeast to this well.
3. Select the gluten-free or basic Bread cycle, and adjust the crust to your preferred setting.
4. Add the raisins about 5 minutes before the last kneading cycle ends.
5. Once done, remove the bread from the machine and let it cool before slicing.

Nutritional per Serving: 210 calories, 4g protein, 38g carbohydrates, 5g fat, 2g fiber, 40mg cholesterol, 200mg sodium, 80mg potassium.

Tip: Coat raisins with gluten-free flour to distribute evenly and avoid sinking in dough.

83. Gluten-Free Quinoa Bread

Prep time: 20 minutes | Cook time: 3 hours 30 minutes

1 ½ Pounds Loaf (≈ 12 slices):

- ¾ cup warm water (about 110°F)
- ¼ cup milk alternative (almond, rice, soy)
- 2 tablespoons olive oil
- 2 eggs, beaten
- 1 cup cooked quinoa (cooled)
- 2 ½ cups gluten-free all-purpose flour blend
- 1 teaspoon salt and 3 tablespoons sugar
- 1 tablespoon xanthan gum (if not included in your flour blend)
- 2 teaspoons active dry yeast

2 Pounds Loaf (≈ 16 slices):

- 1 cup warm water (about 110°F)
- ⅓ cup milk alternative (almond, rice, soy)
- 3 tablespoons olive oil
- 3 eggs, beaten
- 1 ⅓ cups cooked quinoa (cooled)
- 3 ⅓ cups gluten-free all-purpose flour blend
- 1 ¼ teaspoons salt and ¼ cup sugar
- 1 ½ tablespoons xanthan gum (if not included in your flour blend)
- 2 ½ teaspoons active dry yeast

Directions:

1. In a bowl, whisk together the water, milk alternative, olive oil, and beaten eggs. Stir in the cooked quinoa until well combined. Add this mixture to the bread machine pan.
2. Over this, layer the gluten-free flour blend, salt, sugar, and xanthan gum (if using), ensuring not to let the yeast touch the liquid.
3. Make a small well in the center of the dry ingredients and add the yeast.
4. Select the gluten-free or basic Bread cycle, and adjust the crust to your preferred setting.
5. Once done, remove the bread from the machine and let it cool before slicing.

Nutritional per Serving: 180 calories, 5g protein, 30g carbohydrates, 4g fat, 2g fiber, 30mg cholesterol, 200mg sodium, 100mg potassium.

Tip: Toast quinoa flour on a baking sheet at 350°F (175°C) for 5-7 minutes to enhance its nutty flavor without burning.

84. Gluten-Free Rice Bread

Prep time: 20 minutes | Cook time: 3 hours 40 minutes

1 ½ Pounds Loaf (≈ 12 slices):

- 1 cup warm water (about 110°F)
- ¼ cup olive oil
- 3 eggs
- 2 cups gluten-free rice flour
- 1 cup tapioca flour
- ¼ cup sugar and 1 teaspoon salt
- 1 tablespoon xanthan gum (if not included in your flour blend)
- 2 teaspoons active dry yeast

2 Pounds Loaf (≈ 16 slices):

- 1 ⅓ cups warm water (about 110°F)
- ⅓ cup olive oil
- 4 eggs
- 2 ⅔ cups gluten-free rice flour
- 1 ⅓ cups tapioca flour
- ⅓ cup sugar and 1 ¼ teaspoons salt
- 1 ½ tablespoons xanthan gum (if not included in your flour blend)
- 2 ½ teaspoons active dry yeast

Directions:

1. In a bowl, whisk together the warm water, olive oil, and eggs (or flax eggs). Pour this mixture into the bread machine pan.
2. Add the rice flour, tapioca flour, sugar, salt, and xanthan gum over the liquid. Ensure the dry ingredients fully cover the liquid.
3. Make a small well in the center of the dry ingredients (but not deep enough to reach the liquid) and carefully add the yeast to this well.
4. Select the gluten-free or basic Bread cycle, and adjust the crust to your preferred setting.
5. Once done, remove the bread from the machine and let it cool before slicing.

Nutritional per Serving: 210 calories, 3g protein, 38g carbohydrates, 6g fat, 1g fiber, 55mg cholesterol, 200mg sodium, 50mg potassium.

Tip: For a slightly nuttier flavor and additional nutrients, consider substituting ½ cup of rice flour with almond flour. This substitution can add a pleasant texture and richness to the bread.

C. Keto Bread Recipes

85. Keto Almond Flour Bread

Prep time: 10 minutes | Cook time: 2 hours 50 minutes

1 ½ Pounds Loaf (≈ 12 slices):

- 1 ½ cups almond flour
- 5 tablespoons psyllium husk powder
- 2 teaspoons baking powder
- 1 teaspoon salt
- 2 tablespoons coconut oil, melted
- 4 large eggs
- 1 cup warm water (about 110°F)
- 1 teaspoon apple cider vinegar
- 2 teaspoons active dry yeast

2 Pounds Loaf (≈ 16 slices):

- 2 cups almond flour
- 6 tablespoons psyllium husk powder
- 2 ½ teaspoons baking powder
- 1 ¼ teaspoons salt
- 2 ½ tablespoons coconut oil, melted
- 5 large eggs
- 1 ¼ cups warm water
- 1 ½ teaspoons apple cider vinegar
- 2 ½ teaspoons active dry yeast

Directions:

1. In a medium bowl, mix together the almond flour, psyllium husk powder, baking powder, and salt. In another bowl, whisk together the melted coconut oil, eggs, warm water, and apple cider vinegar. Then combine the wet and dry ingredients until a dough forms.
2. Sprinkle the yeast over the dough and gently fold it in, ensuring it's evenly distributed.
3. Transfer the dough to the bread machine pan. Use a spatula to smooth the top.
4. Select the gluten-free or basic Bread cycle, and adjust the crust to your preferred setting.
5. Once done, remove the bread from the machine and let it cool before slicing.

Nutritional per Serving: 190 calories, 7g protein, 8g carbohydrates, 15g fat, 5g fiber, 70mg cholesterol, 220mg sodium, 30mg potassium.

Tip: For a lighter texture, make sure to use finely ground almond flour.

86. Keto Coconut Flour Bread

Prep time: 15 minutes | Cook time: 2 hours 50 minutes

1 ½ Pounds Loaf (≈ 12 slices):

- ¾ cup coconut flour
- ⅓ cup ground flaxseed
- ½ teaspoon salt
- 1 teaspoon baking powder
- 6 large eggs
- ½ cup unsalted butter, melted
- 1 tablespoon apple cider vinegar
- 2 teaspoons active dry yeast
- ½ cup warm water (about 110°F)
- 2 tablespoons erythritol (or another for keto)

2 Pounds Loaf (≈ 16 slices):

- 1 cup coconut flour
- ½ cup ground flaxseed
- ¾ teaspoon salt
- 1 ½ teaspoons baking powder
- 8 large eggs
- ⅔ cup unsalted butter, melted
- 1 ½ tablespoons apple cider vinegar
- 2 ½ teaspoons active dry yeast
- ⅔ cup warm water
- 3 tablespoons erythritol (or another for keto)

Directions:

1. Whisk coconut flour, flaxseed, salt, and baking powder in a large bowl. Beat eggs, mix in melted butter and apple cider vinegar in another bowl.
2. Dissolve erythritol and yeast in warm water and let sit until frothy (5-10 minutes).
3. Mix yeast with egg mixture, then add dry ingredients until combined.
4. Transfer the dough to the bread machine pan. Use a spatula to smooth the top.
5. Select the gluten-free or basic Bread cycle, and adjust the crust to your preferred setting.
6. Once done, remove the bread from the machine and let it cool before slicing.

Nutritional per Serving: 200 calories, 7g protein, 9g carbohydrates, 16g fat, 6g fiber, 140mg cholesterol, 200mg sodium, 50mg potassium.

Tip: Mix in ¼ cup unsweetened almond milk for softer, moister bread with a classic texture.

87. Keto Flaxseed Bread

Prep time: 15 minutes | Cook time: 2 hours 55 minutes

1 ½ Pounds Loaf (≈ 12 slices):

- 1 cup warm water (about 110°F)
- 3 tablespoons coconut oil, melted
- 5 large eggs
- 2 cups ground flaxseed meal
- ½ cup almond flour
- 1 tablespoon baking powder
- ½ teaspoon salt
- 2 teaspoons active dry yeast
- 1 tablespoon erythritol (or another for keto)

2 Pounds Loaf (≈ 16 slices):

- 1 ⅓ cups warm water (about 110°F)
- ¼ cup coconut oil, melted
- 6 large eggs
- 2 ⅔ cups ground flaxseed meal
- ⅔ cup almond flour
- 1 ½ tablespoons baking powder
- ¾ teaspoon salt
- 2 ½ teaspoons active dry yeast
- 1 ½ tablespoons erythritol (or another for keto)

Directions:

1. Whisk warm water, melted coconut oil, and eggs in a large bowl. Mix ground flaxseed, almond flour, baking powder, salt, and erythritol in another bowl.
2. Gradually combine the wet ingredients with the dry ingredients until well incorporated.
3. Dissolve yeast in a small amount of warm water, let froth for 5-10 minutes, then stir into batter.
4. Transfer the mixture into the bread machine pan, smoothing the top with a spatula.
5. Select the gluten-free or basic Bread cycle, and adjust the crust to your preferred setting.
6. Once done, remove the bread from the machine and let it cool before slicing.

Nutritional per Serving: 220 calories, 9g protein, 8g carbohydrates, 18g fat, 6g fiber, 160mg cholesterol, 220mg sodium, 180mg potassium.

Tip: For an extra nutritional boost, consider adding a tablespoon of chia seeds or hemp seeds to the batter for added texture and omega-3 fatty acids.

88. Cheesy Keto Bread

Prep time: 15 minutes | Cook time: 2 hours 45 minutes

1 ½ Pounds Loaf (≈ 12 slices):

- 1 cup warm water (about 110°F)
- ¼ cup unsalted butter, melted
- 3 large eggs
- 2 cups almond flour and ½ cup coconut flour
- ¼ cup ground flaxseed
- 1 teaspoon salt
- 1 tablespoon baking powder
- 2 teaspoons active dry yeast
- 1 cup shredded cheddar cheese
- ½ cup grated Parmesan cheese

2 Pounds Loaf (≈ 16 slices):

- 1 ⅓ cups warm water (about 110°F)
- ⅓ cup unsalted butter, melted
- 4 large eggs
- 2 ⅔ cups almond flour and ⅔ cup coconut flour
- ⅓ cup ground flaxseed
- 1 ¼ teaspoons salt
- 1 ½ tablespoons baking powder
- 2 ½ teaspoons active dry yeast
- 1 ⅓ cups shredded cheddar cheese
- ⅔ cup grated Parmesan cheese

Directions:

1. Mix warm water, melted butter, and eggs in a large bowl. Combine almond flour, coconut flour, ground flaxseed, salt, and baking powder in another bowl.
2. Stir dry ingredients into wet until combined, then fold in cheddar and Parmesan.
3. Dissolve yeast in warm water, let sit, then add to mix.
4. Place dough in bread machine pan, smooth top.
5. Select the gluten-free or basic Bread cycle, and adjust the crust to your preferred setting.
6. Cool bread on a wire rack before slicing.

Nutritional per Serving: 260 calories, 10g protein, 8g carbohydrates, 22g fat, 4g fiber, 90mg cholesterol, 320mg sodium, 100mg potassium.

Tip: For an enhanced flavor profile, consider adding a teaspoon of garlic powder or dried herbs to the dough mixture.

89. Keto Olive Bread

Prep time: 20 minutes | Cook time: 3 hours

1 ½ Pounds Loaf (≈ 12 slices):

- 1 cup warm water (about 110°F)
- ¼ cup olive oil
- 3 large eggs
- 2 cups almond flour and ½ cup coconut flour
- ¼ cup ground flaxseed
- 1 teaspoon salt
- 1 tablespoon baking powder
- 2 teaspoons active dry yeast
- ½ cup chopped kalamata olives
- 1 tablespoon dried rosemary

2 Pounds Loaf (≈ 16 slices):

- 1 ⅓ cups warm water (about 110°F)
- ⅓ cup olive oil
- 4 large eggs
- 2 ⅔ cups almond flour and ⅔ cup coconut flour
- ⅓ cup ground flaxseed
- 1 ¼ teaspoons salt
- 1 ½ tablespoons baking powder
- 2 ½ teaspoons active dry yeast
- ⅔ cup chopped kalamata olives
- 1 ½ tablespoons dried rosemary

Directions:

1. Whisk warm water, olive oil, and eggs in a large bowl. Mix almond flour, coconut flour, ground flaxseed, salt, baking powder, and rosemary in another bowl.
2. Combine dry ingredients with wet, fold in olives, and then sprinkle and fold in yeast.
3. Put dough in bread machine pan, smooth top.
4. Transfer the dough to the bread machine pan, smoothing the top with a spatula.
5. Select the gluten-free or basic Bread cycle, and adjust the crust to your preferred setting.
6. Once done, remove the bread from the machine and let it cool before slicing.

Nutritional per Serving: 280 calories, 9g protein, 8g carbohydrates, 24g fat, 5g fiber, 80mg cholesterol, 340mg sodium, 130mg potassium.

Tip: To enhance the flavor, you can mix in a teaspoon of lemon zest or swap the dried rosemary for fresh if available.

90. Keto High Fiber Bread

Prep time: 20 minutes | Cook time: 3 hours

1 ½ Pounds Loaf (≈ 12 slices):

- 1 cup warm water (about 110°F)
- ¼ cup olive oil
- 3 large eggs
- 2 cups almond flour and ½ cup coconut flour
- ¼ cup psyllium husk powder
- ¼ cup ground flaxseed
- 1 teaspoon salt
- 1 tablespoon baking powder
- 2 teaspoons active dry yeast

2 Pounds Loaf (≈ 16 slices):

- 1 ⅓ cups warm water (about 110°F)
- ⅓ cup olive oil
- 4 large eggs
- 2 ⅔ cups almond flour and ⅔ cup coconut flour
- ⅓ cup psyllium husk powder
- ⅓ cup ground flaxseed
- 1 ¼ teaspoons salt
- 1 ½ tablespoons baking powder
- 2 ½ teaspoons active dry yeast

Directions:

1. Combine the warm water, olive oil, and eggs in a large bowl and whisk together. In a separate bowl, mix the almond flour, coconut flour, psyllium husk powder, ground flaxseed, salt, and baking powder.
2. Gradually mix the wet ingredients into the dry until a dough forms.
3. Add the yeast to the dough, mixing gently to incorporate.
4. Transfer the dough to the bread machine pan, smoothing the top with a spatula.
5. Select the gluten-free or basic Bread cycle, and adjust the crust to your preferred setting.
6. Once done, remove the bread from the machine and let it cool before slicing.

Nutritional per Serving: 290 calories, 10g protein, 12g carbohydrates, 25g fat, 10g fiber, 85mg cholesterol, 350mg sodium, 140mg potassium.

Tip: For a nuttier flavor and extra fiber, consider adding a handful of chopped nuts or seeds to the dough before baking.

D. Low-Carb Bread Recipes

91. *Psyllium Husk Bread*

Prep time: 15 minutes | Cook time: 2 hours 50 minutes

1 ½ Pounds Loaf (≈ 12 slices):

- 1 cup warm water (about 110°F)
- 2 tablespoons olive oil
- 3 large eggs
- 1 ½ cups almond flour and ¾ cup coconut flour
- ¼ cup psyllium husk powder
- 1 teaspoon salt
- 1 tablespoon baking powder
- 2 teaspoons active dry yeast

2 Pounds Loaf (≈ 16 slices):

- 1 ⅓ cups warm water (about 110°F)
- 3 tablespoons olive oil
- 4 large eggs
- 2 cups almond flour and 1 cup coconut flour
- ⅓ cup psyllium husk powder
- 1 ¼ teaspoons salt
- 1 ½ tablespoons baking powder
- 2 ½ teaspoons active dry yeast

Directions:

1. Whisk together the warm water, olive oil, and eggs in a large bowl. In a separate bowl, combine the almond flour, coconut flour, psyllium husk powder, salt, and baking powder.
2. Gradually add the wet ingredients to the dry ingredients, stirring until a dough forms.
3. Sprinkle the yeast over the dough and fold gently to incorporate evenly.
4. Transfer the dough to the bread machine pan and smooth the top with a spatula.
5. Select the gluten-free or basic Bread cycle, and adjust the crust to your preferred setting.
6. Once done, remove the bread from the machine and let it cool before slicing.

Nutritional per Serving: 220 calories, 8g protein, 10g carbohydrates, 18g fat, 9g fiber, 70mg cholesterol, 300mg sodium, 100mg potassium.

Tip: For a smoother texture, ensure the psyllium husk powder is finely ground. This bread is perfect for toasting and can be customized with herbs or spices for added flavor.

92. *Almond Flour Sesame Seed Bread*

Prep time: 20 minutes | Cook time: 3 hours

1 ½ Pounds Loaf (≈ 12 slices):

- 1 cup warm water (about 110°F)
- ¼ cup olive oil
- 3 large eggs
- 2 cups almond flour and ½ cup coconut flour
- ¼ cup ground flaxseed
- 2 tablespoons sesame seeds and topping
- 1 teaspoon salt
- 1 tablespoon baking powder
- 2 teaspoons active dry yeast

2 Pounds Loaf (≈ 16 slices):

- 1 ⅓ cups warm water (about 110°F)
- ⅓ cup olive oil
- 4 large eggs
- 2 ⅔ cups almond flour and ⅔ cup coconut flour
- ⅓ cup ground flaxseed
- 3 tablespoons sesame seeds and topping
- 1 ¼ teaspoons salt
- 1 ½ tablespoons baking powder
- 2 ½ teaspoons active dry yeast

Directions:

1. Mix the warm water, olive oil, and eggs in a bowl until well combined. In a separate bowl, blend the almond flour, coconut flour, ground flaxseed, sesame seeds, salt, and baking powder.
2. Gradually add the wet ingredients to the dry ingredients, stirring until a dough forms.
3. Gently stir in the yeast, ensuring it's evenly distributed throughout the dough.
4. Place the dough in the bread machine pan and smooth the top. Sprinkle additional sesame seeds over the dough for a crunchy topping.
5. Select the gluten-free or basic Bread cycle, and adjust the crust to your preferred setting.
6. Once done, remove the bread from the machine and let it cool before slicing.

Nutritional per Serving: 250 calories, 9g protein, 12g carbohydrates, 20g fat, 6g fiber, 80mg cholesterol, 310mg sodium, 120mg potassium.

Tip: For an extra sesame flavor, consider lightly toasting the sesame seeds before adding them to the dough.

93. Almond Flour Rosemary Bread

Prep time: 15 minutes | Cook time: 2 hours 55 minutes

1 ½ Pounds Loaf (≈ 12 slices):

- 1 cup warm water (about 110°F)
- ¼ cup olive oil
- 3 large eggs
- 2 cups almond flour and ½ cup coconut flour
- ¼ cup ground flaxseed
- 2 tablespoons fresh rosemary, finely chopped, plus extra for topping
- 1 teaspoon salt
- 1 tablespoon baking powder
- 2 teaspoons active dry yeast

2 Pounds Loaf (≈ 16 slices):

- 1 ⅓ cups warm water (about 110°F)
- ⅓ cup olive oil
- 4 large eggs
- 2 ⅔ cups almond flour and ⅔ cup coconut flour
- ⅓ cup ground flaxseed
- 3 tablespoons fresh rosemary, finely chopped, plus extra for topping
- 1 ¼ teaspoons salt
- 1 ½ tablespoons baking powder
- 2 ½ teaspoons active dry yeast

Directions:

1. Whisk warm water, olive oil, and eggs in a bowl. Mix almond flour, coconut flour, ground flaxseed, rosemary, salt, and baking powder in another bowl.
2. Gradually mix wet into dry ingredients until dough is consistent.
3. Fold yeast into dough for even distribution.
4. Place dough in bread machine pan, smooth top, and sprinkle rosemary on top.
5. Select the gluten-free or basic Bread cycle, and adjust the crust to your preferred setting.
6. Once done, remove the bread from the machine and let it cool before slicing.

Nutritional per Serving: 240 calories, 8g protein, 10g carbohydrates, 19g fat, 5g fiber, 75mg cholesterol, 300mg sodium, 100mg potassium.

Tip: To enhance the rosemary flavor, gently bruise the leaves before chopping to release their essential oils.

94. Flaxseed Pecan Bread

Prep time: 20 minutes | Cook time: 3 hours

1 ½ Pounds Loaf (≈ 12 slices):

- 1 cup warm water (about 110°F)
- ¼ cup olive oil
- 3 large eggs
- 2 cups almond flour and ¼ cup coconut flour
- ½ cup ground flaxseed
- ½ cup chopped pecans
- 1 teaspoon salt
- 1 tablespoon baking powder
- 2 teaspoons active dry yeast

2 Pounds Loaf (≈ 16 slices):

- 1 ⅓ cups warm water (about 110°F)
- ⅓ cup olive oil
- 4 large eggs
- 2 ⅔ cups almond flour and ⅓ cup coconut flour
- ⅔ cup ground flaxseed
- ⅔ cup chopped pecans
- 1 ¼ teaspoons salt
- 1 ½ tablespoons baking powder
- 2 ½ teaspoons active dry yeast

Directions:

1. Whisk together the warm water, olive oil, and eggs in a large bowl. In a separate bowl, combine the almond flour, ground flaxseed, coconut flour, chopped pecans, salt, and baking powder.
2. Gradually incorporate the wet mixture into the dry ingredients until a dough forms.
3. Sprinkle the yeast over the mixture and fold gently to evenly distribute.
4. Transfer the dough to the bread machine pan, smoothing the top with a spatula.
5. Select the gluten-free or basic Bread cycle, and adjust the crust to your preferred setting.
6. Once done, remove the bread from the machine and let it cool before slicing.

Nutritional per Serving: 320 calories, 9g protein, 12g carbohydrates, 27g fat, 7g fiber, 80mg cholesterol, 320mg sodium, 150mg potassium.

Tip: Toasting the pecans before adding them to the dough can enhance their flavor and add a delightful crunch to the bread.

95. Low-Carb Anise Bread

Prep Time: 15 minutes | Cook Time: 2 hours 30 minutes

1 ½ Pounds Loaf (≈ 12 slices):

- cup warm water (about 110°F)
- ¼ cup olive oil
- 3 large eggs
- 2 cups almond flour
- ½ cup coconut flour
- ¼ cup flaxseed meal
- 1 teaspoon salt
- 2 teaspoons active dry yeast
- 2 tablespoons anise seeds
- 1 tablespoon erythritol

2 Pounds Loaf (≈ 16 slices):

- 1 ⅓ cups warm water (about 110°F)
- ⅓ cup olive oil
- 4 large eggs
- 2 ⅔ cups almond flour
- ⅔ cup coconut flour
- ⅓ cup flaxseed meal
- 1 ⅓ teaspoon salt
- 2 ½ teaspoons active dry yeast
- 2 ⅔ tablespoons anise seeds
- 1 ⅓ tablespoon erythritol

Directions:

1. Whisk warm water, olive oil, and eggs in a large bowl. Mix almond flour, coconut flour, flaxseed meal, salt, anise seeds, and erythritol in another bowl.
2. Gradually incorporate the wet mixture into the dry ingredients until a dough forms.
3. Sprinkle the yeast over the mixture and fold gently to evenly distribute.
4. Transfer the dough to the bread machine pan. Use a spatula to smooth the top.
5. Select the gluten-free or basic Bread cycle, and adjust the crust to your preferred setting.
6. Once done, remove the bread from the machine and let it cool before slicing.

Nutritional per Serving: 210 calories, 7g protein, 9g carbohydrates, 16g fat, 6g fiber, 95mg cholesterol, 210mg sodium, 110mg potassium.

Tip: Toast anise seeds lightly to enhance their sweet, licorice-like flavor before adding to dough.

96. Low-Carb Honey Bread

Prep Time: 15 minutes | Cook Time: 2 hours 30 minutes

1 ½ Pounds Loaf (≈ 12 slices):

- 1 cup warm water (about 110°F)
- ¼ cup olive oil
- 3 large eggs
- 2 cups almond flour
- ½ cup coconut flour
- ¼ cup flaxseed meal
- 1 teaspoon salt
- 2 teaspoons active dry yeast
- 2 tablespoons anise seeds
- 1 tablespoon erythritol

2 Pounds Loaf (≈ 16 slices):

- 1 ⅓ cups warm water (about 110°F)
- ⅓ cup olive oil
- 4 large eggs
- 2 ⅔ cups almond flour
- ⅔ cup coconut flour
- ⅓ cup flaxseed meal
- 1 ⅓ teaspoon salt
- 2 ½ teaspoons active dry yeast
- 2 ⅔ tablespoons anise seeds
- 1 ⅓ tablespoon erythritol

Directions:

1. Whisk warm water, olive oil, and eggs in a large bowl. Mix almond flour, coconut flour, flaxseed meal, salt, anise seeds, and erythritol in another bowl.
2. Gradually incorporate the wet mixture into the dry ingredients until a dough forms.
3. Sprinkle the yeast over the mixture and fold gently to evenly distribute.
4. Transfer the dough to the bread machine pan. Use a spatula to smooth the top.
5. Select the gluten-free or basic Bread cycle, and adjust the crust to your preferred setting.
6. Once done, remove the bread from the machine and let it cool before slicing.

Nutritional per Serving: 220 calories, 8g protein, 10g carbohydrates, 18g fat, 6g fiber, 85mg cholesterol, 220mg sodium, 100mg potassium.

Tip: For stricter carb control, replace honey with a low-carb sweetener, adjusting liquid as needed.

Chapter 10: Quick Bread

A. Sweet Quick Bread Recipes

97. Vanilla Quick Bread

Prep Time: 15 minutes | Cook Time: 1 hour 30 minutes

1 ½ Pounds Loaf (≈ 12 slices):

- 1 ¾ cups all-purpose flour
- ⅔ cup granulated sugar and ½ teaspoon salt
- 2 teaspoons baking powder
- 1 cup lukewarm milk
- ¼ cup unsalted butter, melted
- 2 large eggs
- 2 teaspoons vanilla extract

2 Pounds Loaf (≈ 16 slices):

- 2 ⅓ cups all-purpose flour
- 1 cup granulated sugar and ⅔ teaspoon salt
- 2 ⅔ teaspoons baking powder
- 1 ⅓ cups lukewarm milk
- ⅓ cup unsalted butter, melted
- 3 large eggs
- 2 ⅔ teaspoons vanilla extract

Directions:

1. In a large mixing bowl, whisk together the flour, sugar, baking powder, and salt.
2. In a separate bowl, mix together the milk, melted butter, eggs, and vanilla extract until well combined.
3. Gradually add the wet ingredients to the dry ingredients, stirring until just combined. Be careful not to overmix.
4. Pour the batter into the bread machine pan.
5. Select the "Quick Bread" or "Cake" cycle on your bread machine.
6. Once done, remove the bread from the machine and let it cool before slicing.

Nutritional per Serving: 210 calories, 5g protein, 34g carbohydrates, 6g fat, 1g fiber, 55mg cholesterol, 210mg sodium, 90mg potassium.

Tip: Boost vanilla flavor by adding seeds from a vanilla bean pod and extract to the batter for delicious taste and visual appeal.

98. Chocolate Quick Bread

Prep Time: 15 minutes | Cook Time: 1 hour 20 minutes

1 ½ Pounds Loaf (≈ 12 slices):

- 1 ½ cups all-purpose flour
- ½ cup unsweetened cocoa powder
- ¾ cup granulated sugar and ¼ teaspoon salt
- 1 teaspoon baking powder
- ½ teaspoon baking soda
- 1 cup buttermilk
- 2 large eggs
- 1 teaspoon vanilla extract
- ½ cup semi-sweet chocolate chips

2 Pounds Loaf (≈ 16 slices):

- 2 cups all-purpose flour
- ⅔ cup unsweetened cocoa powder
- 1 cup granulated sugar and ⅓ teaspoon salt
- 1 ⅓ teaspoons baking powder
- ⅔ teaspoon baking soda
- 1 ⅓ cups buttermilk
- ⅓ cup vegetable oil
- 3 large eggs
- 1 ⅓ teaspoons vanilla extract
- ⅔ cup semi-sweet chocolate chips

Directions:

1. In a large mixing bowl, sift together the flour, cocoa powder, sugar, baking powder, baking soda, and salt. In a separate bowl, whisk together the buttermilk, vegetable oil, eggs, and vanilla extract until well combined.
2. Gradually mix wet into dry ingredients until just combined; avoid overmixing.
3. Fold in the chocolate chips gently.
4. Pour the batter into the bread machine pan.
5. Select the "Quick Bread" or "Cake" cycle on your bread machine.
6. Once done, remove the bread from the machine and let it cool before slicing.

Nutritional per Serving: 230 calories, 5g protein, 35g carbohydrates, 9g fat, 2g fiber, 45mg cholesterol, 190mg sodium, 120mg potassium.

Tip: For an extra rich chocolate flavor, consider using a combination of cocoa powder and melted dark chocolate in the batter. This intensifies the chocolate flavor and adds moisture to the bread.

99. Brown Sugar Pecan Bread

Prep Time: 15 minutes | Cook Time: 1 hours 20 minutes

1 ½ Pounds Loaf (≈ 12 slices):

- 2 cups all-purpose flour
- ¾ cup brown sugar, packed + for topping
- 1 teaspoon baking powder
- ½ teaspoon baking soda
- ¼ teaspoon salt
- ½ cup milk
- ¼ cup unsalted butter, melted
- 2 large eggs
- 1 teaspoon vanilla extract
- ½ cup chopped pecans

2 Pounds Loaf (≈ 16 slices):

- 2 ⅔ cups all-purpose flour
- 1 cup brown sugar, packed + for topping
- 1 ⅓ teaspoons baking powder
- ⅔ teaspoon baking soda
- ⅓ teaspoon salt
- ⅔ cup milk
- ⅓ cup unsalted butter, melted
- 3 large eggs
- 1 ⅓ teaspoons vanilla extract
- ⅔ cup chopped pecans

Directions:

1. Mix flour, brown sugar, baking powder, baking soda, and salt in a large bowl. Whisk milk, melted butter, eggs, and vanilla extract in another bowl.
2. Gradually incorporate the wet mixture into the dry ingredients until a dough forms.
3. Fold in the chopped pecans.
4. Pour batter into pan; sprinkle with brown sugar on top for crunch, if using.
5. Select the "Quick Bread" or "Cake" cycle on your bread machine.
6. Once done, remove the bread from the machine and let it cool before slicing.

Nutritional per Serving: 220 calories, 5g protein, 32g carbohydrates, 9g fat, 2g fiber, 45mg cholesterol, 180mg sodium, 110mg potassium.

Tip: Sprinkle brown sugar and crushed pecans over batter before starting the machine for a crunchy top and nutty flavor.

100. Raisin Quick Bread

Prep Time: 15 minutes | Cook Time: 1 hours 30 minutes

1 ½ Pounds Loaf (≈ 12 slices):

- 2 cups all-purpose flour
- 1 cup granulated sugar and ½ teaspoon salt
- 1 ½ tcaspoons baking powder
- ½ teaspoon baking soda
- 1 teaspoon cinnamon
- ¾ cup milk
- ¼ cup vegetable oil
- 2 large eggs
- 1 teaspoon vanilla extract
- 1 cup raisins

2 Pounds Loaf (≈ 16 slices):

- 2 ⅔ cups all-purpose flour
- 1 ⅓ cups granulated sugar and ⅔ teaspoon salt
- 2 teaspoons baking powder
- ⅔ teaspoon baking soda
- 1 ⅓ teaspoons cinnamon
- 1 cup milk
- ⅓ cup vegetable oil
- 3 large eggs
- 1 ⅓ teaspoons vanilla extract
- 1 ⅓ cups raisins

Directions:

1. Whisk flour, sugar, baking powder, baking soda, salt, and cinnamon in a large bowl. Combine milk, oil, eggs, and vanilla in another bowl and mix well.
2. Gradually incorporate the wet mixture into the dry ingredients until a dough forms.
3. Fold in the raisins gently.
4. Pour the batter into the bread machine pan.
5. Select the "Quick Bread" or "Cake" cycle on your bread machine.
6. Once done, remove the bread from the machine and let it cool before slicing.

Nutritional per Serving: 210 calories, 4g protein, 37g carbohydrates, 5g fat, 1g fiber, 40mg cholesterol, 180mg sodium, 120mg potassium.

Tip: Soak the raisins in warm water or orange juice for 10 minutes before adding them to the batter to plump them up and add extra moisture and flavor to the bread.

B. Fruit Quick Bread Recipes

101. *Cherry Almond Quick Bread*

Prep Time: 15 minutes | Cook Time: 1 hour 30 minutes

1 ½ Pounds Loaf (≈ 12 slices):

- 1 ¾ cups all-purpose flour
- ¾ cup sugar and ½ teaspoon salt
- 2 teaspoons baking powder
- ⅓ cup unsalted butter, melted
- ¾ cup milk
- 2 large eggs
- 1 teaspoon almond extract
- 1 cup dried cherries, chopped
- ½ cup slivered almonds

2 Pounds Loaf (≈ 16 slices):

- 2 ⅓ cups all-purpose flour
- 1 cup sugar and ⅔ teaspoon salt
- 2 ½ teaspoons baking powder
- ½ cup unsalted butter, melted
- 1 cup milk
- 3 large eggs
- 1 ⅓ teaspoons almond extract
- 1 ⅓ cups dried cherries, chopped
- ⅔ cup slivered almonds

Directions:

1. Soak dried cherries in warm water for 10 mins, then drain.
2. Whisk flour, sugar, baking powder, and salt in a large bowl. Mix melted butter, milk, eggs, and almond extract in another bowl.
3. Gradually combine wet and dry ingredients until just mixed; avoid overmixing for tender bread. Gently fold in the plumped cherries and slivered almonds into the batter.
4. Pour the batter into the bread machine pan.
5. Select the "Quick Bread" or "Cake" cycle on your bread machine.
6. Once done, remove the bread from the machine and let it cool before slicing.

Nutritional per Serving: 230 calories, 5g protein, 38g carbohydrates, 8g fat, 2g fiber, 55mg cholesterol, 200mg sodium, 120mg potassium.

Tip: Lightly toast slivered almonds before adding to batter for a richer taste and extra crunch.

102. *Peach Bread Quick Bread*

Prep Time: 15 minutes | Cook Time: 1 hour 20 minutes

1 ½ Pounds Loaf (≈ 12 slices):

- 1 ½ cups all-purpose flour
- ¾ cup granulated sugar
- ½ teaspoon salt
- 2 teaspoons baking powder
- ⅓ cup vegetable oil
- 2 large eggs, beaten
- 1 teaspoon vanilla extract
- 1 cup fresh peaches, peeled and diced
- ½ cup sour cream or Greek yogurt

2 Pounds Loaf (≈ 16 slices):

- 2 cups all-purpose flour
- 1 cup granulated sugar
- ⅔ teaspoon salt
- 2 ⅔ teaspoons baking powder
- ½ cup vegetable oil
- 3 large eggs, beaten
- 1 ⅓ teaspoons vanilla extract
- 1 ⅓ cups fresh peaches, peeled and diced
- ⅔ cup sour cream or Greek yogurt

Directions:

1. In a large mixing bowl, whisk together the flour, sugar, salt, and baking powder.
2. In another bowl, mix the vegetable oil, eggs, and vanilla extract. Stir in the sour cream (or Greek yogurt) until well combined.
3. Gradually incorporate the wet mixture into the dry ingredients until a dough forms.
4. Gently fold in the diced peaches.
5. Pour the batter into the bread machine pan.
6. Select the "Quick Bread" or "Cake" setting on your bread machine.
7. Once done, remove the bread from the machine and let it cool before slicing.

Nutritional per Serving: 210 calories, 4g protein, 30g carbohydrates, 9g fat, 1g fiber, 55mg cholesterol, 200mg sodium, 100mg potassium.

Tip: For an extra burst of flavor, you can mix in a tablespoon of peach preserves into your batter. It not only adds sweetness but also intensifies the peachy flavor, making each slice irresistibly moist and delicious.

103. Dry Cranberry Quick Bread

Prep Time: 10 minutes | Cook Time: 1 hour 20 minutes

1 ½ Pounds Loaf (≈ 12 slices):

- 1 ¾ cups all-purpose flour
- ¾ cup granulated sugar and ½ teaspoon salt
- 2 teaspoons baking powder
- ½ cup unsalted butter, melted
- 2 large eggs
- 1 teaspoon vanilla extract
- ½ cup milk
- 1 cup dry cranberries
- ½ cup chopped walnuts (optional)

2 Pounds Loaf (≈ 16 slices):

- 2 ⅓ cups all-purpose flour
- 1 cup granulated sugar and ⅔ teaspoon salt
- 2 ⅔ teaspoons baking powder
- ⅔ cup unsalted butter, melted
- 3 large eggs
- 1 ⅓ teaspoons vanilla extract
- ⅔ cup milk
- 1 ⅓ cups dry cranberries
- ⅔ cup chopped walnuts (optional)

Directions:

1. In a large bowl, whisk together the flour, sugar, salt, and baking powder. In a separate bowl, mix the melted butter, eggs, vanilla extract, and milk until well combined.
2. Gradually incorporate the wet ingredients into the dry ingredients, stirring until just combined. Avoid overmixing to keep the bread tender.
3. Gently fold in the dry cranberries and walnuts, if using.
4. Pour the batter into the bread machine pan.
5. Select the "Quick Bread" or "Cake" cycle on your bread machine.
6. Once done, remove the bread from the machine and let it cool before slicing.

Nutritional per Serving: 210 calories, 4g protein, 35g carbohydrates, 8g fat, 2g fiber, 55mg cholesterol, 180mg sodium, 100mg potassium.

Tip: Soak cranberries in warm orange juice or water for 10 minutes before adding to batter to plump them up and add a citrus note.

104. Apple-Pie Bread

Prep Time: 15 minutes | Cook Time: 1 hour 40 minutes

1 ½ Pounds Loaf (≈ 12 slices):

- 2 cups all-purpose flour
- 1 cup granulated sugar, ½ teaspoon salt
- 1 ½ teaspoons baking powder
- ½ teaspoon baking soda
- 2 teaspoons cinnamon
- ½ teaspoon nutmeg
- 2 large eggs
- ½ cup unsalted butter, melted
- 1 teaspoon vanilla extract
- 1 ½ cups diced fresh apples
- ½ cup walnuts, ½ cup raisins (optional)

2 Pounds Loaf (≈ 16 slices):

- 2 ⅔ cups all-purpose flour
- 1 ⅓ cups granulated sugar, ⅔ teaspoon salt
- 2 teaspoons baking powder
- ⅔ teaspoon baking soda
- 2 ⅔ teaspoons cinnamon
- ⅔ teaspoon nutmeg
- 3 large eggs
- ⅔ cup unsalted butter, melted
- 1 ⅓ teaspoons vanilla extract
- 2 cups diced fresh apples
- ⅔ cup walnuts, ⅔ cup raisins (optional)

Directions:

1. In a large bowl, mix together the flour, sugar, baking powder, baking soda, salt, cinnamon, and nutmeg. Beat in the eggs, melted butter, and vanilla extract until well combined.
2. Fold in the diced apples, walnuts, and raisins, if using, until evenly distributed.
3. Pour the batter into the bread machine pan.
4. Select the "Quick Bread" or "Cake" setting on your bread machine.
5. Once done, remove the bread from the machine and let it cool before slicing.

Nutritional per Serving: 220 calories, 4g protein, 32g carbohydrates, 9g fat, 2g fiber, 55mg cholesterol, 190mg sodium, 120mg potassium.

Tip: Sprinkle cinnamon and sugar on the batter before baking for a richer apple flavor and a crust like apple pie topping.

C. Savory Bread Recipes

105. Parmesan-Sage Beer Bread

Prep Time: 10 minutes | Cook Time: 1 hour

1 ½ Pounds Loaf (≈ 12 slices):

- 3 cups all-purpose flour
- 1 tablespoon baking powder
- 1 teaspoon salt
- 1 tablespoon dried sage
- 1 cup freshly grated Parmesan cheese
- 12 ounces beer (any light or amber variety works well)
- ¼ cup unsalted butter, melted

2 Pounds Loaf (≈ 16 slices):

- 4 cups all-purpose flour
- 1 ⅓ tablespoons baking powder
- 1 ⅓ teaspoons salt
- 1 ⅓ tablespoons dried sage
- 1 ⅓ cups freshly grated Parmesan cheese
- 16 ounces beer (any light or amber variety works well)
- ⅓ cup unsalted butter, melted

Directions:

1. Start by lightly greasing the bread pan of your bread machine or lining it with parchment paper if your machine's instructions recommend it for quick breads.
2. In a large bowl, whisk together the flour, baking powder, salt, dried sage, and grated Parmesan cheese.
3. Pour in the beer and add the melted butter to the dry ingredients. Stir until just combined; the batter should be lumpy but well incorporated.
4. Pour the batter into the bread machine pan.
5. Select the "Quick Bread" or "Cake" setting on your bread machine.
6. Once done, remove the bread from the machine and let it cool before slicing.

Nutritional per Serving: 210 calories, 7g protein, 33g carbohydrates, 6g fat, 1g fiber, 15mg cholesterol, 430mg sodium, 95mg potassium.

Tip: The unique combination of beer, Parmesan, and sage offers a rich flavor profile that pairs wonderfully with soups and stews.

106. Zucchini Quick Bread

Prep Time: 15 minutes | Cook Time: 1 hour

1 ½ Pounds Loaf (≈ 12 slices):

- 2 cups all-purpose flour
- 1 cup granulated sugar and ½ teaspoon salt
- 1 ½ teaspoons baking powder
- ½ teaspoon baking soda
- 1 teaspoon cinnamon
- 1 cup grated zucchini (squeezed and drained of excess moisture)
- 2 large eggs
- ½ cup vegetable oil
- 2 teaspoons vanilla extract
- ½ cup chopped nuts (optional)

2 Pounds Loaf (≈ 16 slices):

- 2 ⅔ cups all-purpose flour
- 1 ⅓ cups granulated sugar and ⅔ teaspoon salt
- 2 teaspoons baking powder
- ⅔ teaspoon baking soda
- 1 ⅓ teaspoons cinnamon
- 1 ⅓ cups grated zucchini (squeezed and drained of excess moisture)
- 3 large eggs
- ⅔ cup vegetable oil
- 2 ⅔ teaspoons vanilla extract
- ⅔ cup chopped nuts (optional)

Directions:

1. In a large bowl, mix together flour, sugar, baking powder, baking soda, cinnamon, and salt.
2. Stir in the grated zucchini, eggs, vegetable oil, vanilla extract, and nuts if using until just combined.
3. Pour the batter into the bread machine pan.
4. Select the "Quick Bread" or "Cake" setting. Start the machine.
5. Once done, remove the bread from the machine and let it cool before slicing.

Nutritional per Serving: 200 calories, 4g protein, 30g carbohydrates, 8g fat, 1g fiber, 40mg cholesterol, 200mg sodium, 90mg potassium.

Tip: Keeping some moisture in the zucchini helps make the bread moist. For a delightful breakfast, try toasting slices of this bread and serving with butter or cream cheese.

107. Mushrooms Quick Bread

Prep Time: 25 minutes | Cook Time: 1 hour

1 ½ Pounds Loaf (≈ 12 slices):

- 1 cup finely chopped mushrooms
- 1 tablespoon olive oil
- 1 ½ cups all-purpose flour
- ½ cup whole wheat flour
- 2 teaspoons baking powder
- ½ teaspoon salt and 1 tablespoon sugar
- ¼ teaspoon black pepper
- 3 large eggs
- ¼ cup milk
- ¼ cup unsalted butter, melted

2 Pounds Loaf (≈ 16 slices):

- 1 ⅓ cups finely chopped mushrooms
- 1 ⅓ tablespoon olive oil
- 2 cups all-purpose flour
- ⅔ cup whole wheat flour
- 2 ⅔ teaspoons baking powder
- ⅔ teaspoon salt and 1 ⅓ tablespoons sugar
- ⅓ teaspoon black pepper
- 4 large eggs
- ⅓ cup milk
- ⅓ cup unsalted butter, melted

Directions:

1. Sauté mushrooms in olive oil until tender, about 5-7 minutes, then let cool.
2. In a bowl, mix together the all-purpose flour, whole wheat flour, baking powder, salt, and black pepper. In a separate bowl, beat the eggs, then mix in the milk, melted butter, and sugar. Add the cooled mushrooms.
3. Combine the wet ingredients with the dry ingredients until just mixed.
4. Pour the batter into the bread machine pan.
5. Select the "Quick Bread" or "Cake" setting on your bread machine.
6. Once done, remove the bread from the machine and let it cool before slicing.

Nutritional per Serving: 180 calories, 6g protein, 27g carbohydrates, 5g fat, 2g fiber, 55mg cholesterol, 200mg sodium, 90mg potassium.

Tip: Enhance the bread's umami flavor by using a variety of mushrooms, such as shiitake, oyster, and portobello.

108. Tomato and Herb Quick Bread

Prep time: 15 minutes | Cook time: 1 hour

1 ½ Pounds Loaf (≈ 12 slices):

- 1 cup canned diced tomatoes, drained
- 3 cups all-purpose flour
- 1 tablespoon sugar and 1 teaspoon salt
- 1 ½ teaspoons baking powder
- ½ teaspoon baking soda
- 1 tsp. dried oregano and 1 tsp. dried basil
- ½ teaspoon garlic powder
- ¼ cup olive oil
- 1 egg
- 1 cup buttermilk

2 Pounds Loaf (≈ 16 slices):

- 1 ⅓ cups canned diced tomatoes, drained
- 4 cups all-purpose flour
- 1 ⅓ tablespoons sugar and 1 ⅓ teaspoons salt
- 2 teaspoons baking powder
- ⅔ teaspoon baking soda
- 1 ⅓ tsp. dried oregano and 1 ⅓ tsp. dried basil
- ⅔ teaspoon garlic powder
- ⅓ cup olive oil
- 1 ⅓ eggs (beat 2 eggs and remove a bit)
- 1 ⅓ cups buttermilk

Directions:

1. In the bread machine pan, combine the drained diced tomatoes, all-purpose flour, sugar, baking powder, baking soda, salt, dried oregano, dried basil, and garlic powder.
2. In a separate bowl, whisk together the olive oil, egg, and buttermilk. Add this mixture to the dry ingredients in the bread machine pan.
3. Use a spatula to mix the ingredients until just combined; do not overmix. Smooth the top of the batter with the spatula.
4. Set the bread machine to the "Quick Bread" or similar setting if available. Start the cycle.
5. Once done, remove the bread from the machine and let it cool before slicing.

Nutritional per Serving: 200 calories, 5g protein, 35g carbohydrates, 5g fat, 1g fiber, 20mg cholesterol, 300mg sodium, 100mg potassium.

Tip: For a moister bread, consider adding a tablespoon of tomato paste to the batter.

Chapter 11: Pizza & Focaccia Breads

A. Pizza Bread Recipes

109. Margherita Pizza Bread

Prep time: 15 minutes | Cook time: 3 hours 45 minutes

1 ½ Pounds Loaf (≈ 12 slices):

- 1 cup + 2 tablespoons lukewarm water
- 2 tablespoons olive oil
- 3 cups bread flour
- 1 teaspoon salt and 2 teaspoons sugar
- 1 ½ teaspoons active dry yeast
- 1 teaspoon dried basil
- ½ cup diced tomatoes, drained
- ½ cup shredded mozzarella cheese
- 2 tablespoons grated Parmesan cheese

2 Pounds Loaf (≈ 16 slices):

- 1 ⅓ cups lukewarm water
- 3 tablespoons olive oil
- 4 cups bread flour
- 1 ⅓ teaspoons salt and 2 ⅔ teaspoons sugar
- 2 teaspoons active dry yeast
- 1 ⅓ teaspoons dried basil
- ⅔ cup diced tomatoes, drained
- ⅔ cup shredded mozzarella cheese
- ¼ cup grated Parmesan cheese

Directions:

1. Add water and olive oil to the bread machine pan, then cover with bread flour, to evenly covers the liquid. Sprinkle the salt, sugar, and dried basil over the flour. Create a small well in the center of the flour mixture, add yeast.
2. Select the basic or white Bread cycle, and adjust the crust to your preferred setting.
3. Just before the final kneading cycle ends (≈ 10 min), add the diced tomatoes, shredded mozzarella, and grated Parmesan cheese.
4. Once done, remove the bread from the machine and let it cool before slicing.

Nutritional per Serving: 190 calories, 7g protein, 27g carbohydrates, 5g fat, 1g fiber, 10mg cholesterol, 300mg sodium, 80mg potassium.

Tip: Drain and dry tomatoes to reduce moisture and ensuring ideal bread texture.

110. Pepperoni Pizza Bread

Prep time: 15 minutes | Cook time: 3 hours 30 minutes

1 ½ Pounds Loaf (≈ 12 slices):

- 1 cup + 2 tablespoons lukewarm water
- 2 tablespoons olive oil
- 3 cups bread flour
- 1 teaspoon salt and 1 tablespoon sugar
- 1 ½ teaspoons active dry yeast
- 1 teaspoon garlic powder
- 1 teaspoon dried oregano
- ½ cup pepperoni, chopped
- ½ cup shredded mozzarella cheese
- ¼ cup marinara sauce

2 Pounds Loaf (≈ 16 slices):

- 1 ⅓ cups lukewarm water
- 3 tablespoons olive oil
- 4 cups bread flour
- 1 ⅓ teaspoons salt and 1 ⅓ tablespoons sugar
- 2 teaspoons active dry yeast
- 1 ⅓ teaspoons garlic powder
- 1 ⅓ teaspoons dried oregano
- ⅔ cup pepperoni, chopped
- ⅔ cup shredded mozzarella cheese
- ⅓ cup marinara sauce

Directions:

1. Add water and olive oil to the bread machine pan. Follow with the bread flour, ensuring it covers the liquids. Sprinkle the salt, sugar, garlic powder, and dried oregano on top. Make a small well in the center of the flour mixture, add yeast.
2. Select the basic or white Bread cycle, and adjust the crust to your preferred setting.
3. Just before the final kneading cycle ends (≈ 10 min), add the chopped pepperoni, shredded mozzarella cheese, and marinara sauce over the dough.
4. Once done, remove the bread from the machine and let it cool before slicing.

Nutritional per Serving: 200 calories, 8g protein, 27g carbohydrates, 7g fat, 1g fiber, 15mg cholesterol, 350mg sodium, 100mg potassium.

Tip: For a crispier crust, brush the dough with olive oil before adding the toppings.

111. Four Cheese Pizza Bread

Prep time: 15 minutes | Cook time: 3 hours 40 minutes

1 ½ Pounds Loaf (≈ 12 slices):

- 1 cup + 2 tablespoons lukewarm water
- 2 tablespoons olive oil
- 3 cups bread flour
- 1 tablespoon sugar and 1 teaspoon salt
- 1 ½ teaspoons active dry yeast
- ½ tablespoon garlic powder and
- ½ tablespoon dried oregano
- ¼ cup shredded mozzarella
- ¼ cup shredded cheddar cheese
- ¼ cup grated parmesan cheese
- ¼ cup cubed feta cheese

2 Pounds Loaf (≈ 16 slices):

- 1 ⅓ cups lukewarm water
- 3 tablespoons olive oil
- 4 cups bread flour
- 1 ⅓ tablespoons sugar and 1 ⅓ teaspoons salt
- 2 teaspoons active dry yeast
- ⅔ tablespoon garlic powder and
- ⅔ tablespoon dried oregano
- ⅓ cup shredded mozzarella cheese
- ⅓ cup shredded cheddar cheese
- ⅓ cup grated parmesan cheese
- ⅓ cup cubed feta cheese

Directions:

1. In the bread machine pan, combine water and olive oil. Over this, add bread flour, ensuring it covers the liquids. Sprinkle sugar, salt, garlic powder, and dried oregano on top. Make a well in the center and add the yeast.
2. Select the basic or white Bread cycle, and adjust the crust to your preferred setting.
3. At the add-in beep or just before the final kneading cycle ends (≈ 10 min), pause the machine and add the mozzarella, cheddar, Parmesan, and feta cheeses.
4. Once done, remove the bread from the machine and let it cool before slicing.

Nutritional per Serving: 220 calories, 9g protein, 28g carbohydrates, 8g fat, 1g fiber, 20mg cholesterol, 400mg sodium, 90mg potassium.

Tip: For best flavor, use freshly grated cheeses.

112. Hawaiian Pizza Bread

Prep time: 15 minutes | Cook time: 3 hours 40 minutes

1 ½ Pounds Loaf (≈ 12 slices):

- 1 cup + 2 tablespoons lukewarm water
- 2 tablespoons olive oil
- 3 cups bread flour
- 1 tablespoon sugar and 1 teaspoon salt
- 1 ½ teaspoons active dry yeast
- ½ cup diced ham
- ½ cup pineapple tidbits, drained
- ½ cup shredded mozzarella cheese
- 1 teaspoon dried oregano

2 Pounds Loaf (≈ 16 slices):

- 1 ⅓ cups lukewarm water
- 3 tablespoons olive oil
- 4 cups bread flour
- 1 ⅓ tablespoons sugar and 1 ⅓ teaspoons salt
- 2 teaspoons active dry yeast
- ⅔ cup diced ham
- ⅔ cup pineapple tidbits, drained
- ⅔ cup shredded mozzarella cheese
- 1 ⅓ teaspoons dried oregano

Directions:

1. Place water and olive oil in the bread machine pan. Add the flour, ensuring it fully covers the liquids. Sprinkle the sugar, salt, and dried oregano evenly over the flour. Make a well in the center and add the yeast.
2. Start the bread machine on the Basic or White Bread cycle. Choose your crust preference if your machine has that option.
3. At the add-in signal or just before the final kneading cycle ends (≈ 10 min), gently add the diced ham, drained pineapple tidbits, and shredded mozzarella cheese to the dough.
4. Once done, remove the bread from the machine and let it cool before slicing.

Nutritional per Serving: 200 calories, 5g protein, 35g carbohydrates, 5g fat, 1g fiber, 20mg cholesterol, 300mg sodium; 100mg potassium.

Tip: Press pineapple between paper towels to remove moisture before adding to dough, preventing soggy bread and ensuring perfect texture.

B. Pizza Dough Recipes

113. *Basic Pizza Dough*

Prep time: 10 minutes | Cook time: 1 hour 30 minutes (Dough cycle)

Ingredients for 12-inch pizza:

- 1 cup lukewarm water
- 2 tablespoons olive oil
- 3 cups bread flour
- 1 teaspoon sugar
- 1 teaspoon salt
- 2 ¼ teaspoons active dry yeast

Ingredients for 16-inch pizza:

- 1 ⅓ cups lukewarm water
- 3 tablespoons olive oil
- 4 cups bread flour
- 1 ⅓ teaspoons sugar
- 1 ⅓ teaspoons salt
- 1 tablespoon active dry yeast

Directions:

1. Add the lukewarm water and olive oil to the bread machine pan.
2. Over the liquids, add the bread flour, ensuring it covers the liquid completely. Sprinkle the sugar and salt evenly over the flour. Make a small well in the center of the flour mixture and add the yeast.
3. Select the Dough cycle on your bread machine and start the program.
4. Once the Dough cycle is complete, remove the dough from the bread machine. On a floured surface, knead the dough briefly, then roll out to your desired pizza size.
5. Topped with your favorite ingredients, and baked in a preheated oven at 425°F (220°C) for 15-20 minutes, depending on the toppings and desired crust crispiness or until the cheese is bubbly and golden brown.

Nutritional per Serving: 180 calories, 5g protein, 30g carbohydrates, 4g fat, 1g fiber, 0mg cholesterol, 290mg sodium, 50mg potassium.

Tip: For a crisper crust, preheat your pizza stone or baking sheet in the oven before placing your rolled-out dough on it.

114. *Whole Wheat Pizza Dough*

Prep time: 10 minutes | Cook time: 1 hour 30 minutes (Dough cycle)

Ingredients for 12-inch pizza:

- 1 cup lukewarm water
- 2 tablespoons olive oil
- 2 cups whole wheat flour
- 1 cup bread flour
- 1 teaspoon sugar
- 1 teaspoon salt
- 2 ¼ teaspoons active dry yeast

Ingredients for 16-inch pizza:

- 1 ⅓ cups lukewarm water
- 3 tablespoons olive oil
- 2 ⅔ cups whole wheat flour
- 1 ⅓ cups bread flour
- 1 ⅓ teaspoons sugar
- 1 ⅓ teaspoons salt
- 1 tablespoon active dry yeast

Directions:

1. Pour the lukewarm water and olive oil into the bread machine pan.
2. Add both types of flour to the pan, ensuring they cover the liquid. Sprinkle the sugar and salt evenly over the flour. Make a well in the center and add the yeast.
3. Select the Dough cycle on your bread machine and start it. The machine will mix, knead, and allow the dough to rise.
4. Once the Dough cycle is complete, remove the dough from the bread machine. On a floured surface, knead the dough briefly, then roll out to your desired pizza size
5. Topped with your favorite ingredients, and baked in a preheated oven at 425°F (220°C) for 15-20 minutes, depending on the toppings and desired crust crispiness or until the cheese is bubbly and golden brown.

Nutritional per Serving: 200 calories, 6g protein, 36g carbohydrates, 4.5g fat, 4g fiber, 0mg cholesterol, 290mg sodium, 180mg potassium.

Tip: Let the dough rest for a few minutes after shaping and before adding toppings to allow for easier handling and a lighter crust.

115. Italian Pizza Dough

Prep time: 20 minutes | Cook time: 1 hour 30 minutes (Dough cycle)

Ingredients for 12-inch pizza:

- 1 cup lukewarm water
- 2 tablespoons olive oil
- 3 cups bread flour
- 1 teaspoon salt
- 1 tablespoon sugar
- 2 teaspoons active dry yeast
- 1 teaspoon dried Italian herbs
- 1 crushed garlic clove

2 Pounds Loaf (≈ 16 slices):

- 1 ⅓ cups lukewarm water
- 3 tablespoons olive oil
- 4 cups bread flour
- 1 ⅓ teaspoons salt
- 1 ⅓ tablespoons sugar
- 2 ½ teaspoons active dry yeast
- 1 ⅓ teaspoons dried Italian herbs
- 2 crushed garlic cloves

Directions:

1. Add the lukewarm water, olive oil, and crushed garlic clove(s) to the bread machine pan.
2. Over this, layer the bread flour, making sure to cover the wet ingredients completely. Sprinkle the salt, sugar, and dried Italian herbs evenly over the flour. Make a small indentation in the center of the flour and add the active dry yeast.
3. Select the Dough cycle on your bread machine and start the program.
4. Once the Dough cycle is complete, remove the dough from the bread machine. On a floured surface, knead the dough briefly, then roll out to your desired pizza size.
5. Topped with your favorite ingredients, and baked in a preheated oven at 425°F (220°C) for 15-20 minutes, depending on the toppings and desired crust crispiness or until the cheese is bubbly and golden brown.

Nutritional per Serving: 220 calories, 6g protein, 37g carbohydrates, 5g fat, 2g fiber, 0mg cholesterol, 290mg sodium, 80mg potassium.

Tip: Let dough rest overnight in the fridge after Dough cycle for deeper flavor.

116. Sourdough Pizza Dough

Prep time: 15 minutes | Cook time: 1 hour 30 minutes (Dough cycle)

1 ½ Pounds Loaf (≈ 12 slices):

- ¾ cup sourdough starter, active and bubbly
- ½ cup water, lukewarm
- 2 tablespoons olive oil
- 3 cups bread flour
- 1 teaspoon salt
- 1 teaspoon sugar (optional, helps browning)
- ½ teaspoon active dry yeast (optional, for quicker rise).

2 Pounds Loaf (≈ 16 slices):

- 1 cup sourdough starter, active and bubbly
- ⅔ cup water, lukewarm
- 3 tablespoons olive oil
- 4 cups bread flour
- 1 ⅓ teaspoons salt
- 1 ⅓ teaspoons sugar (optional, helps browning)
- ¾ teaspoon active dry yeast (optional, for quicker rise).

Directions:

1. In the bread machine pan, combine the sourdough starter, lukewarm water, olive oil.
2. Add the bread flour, salt, and sugar over the wet ingredients. If using, sprinkle the active dry yeast last. Make a small indentation in the flour for the yeast to ensure it does not contact the wet ingredients directly.
3. Select the Dough cycle on your bread machine and start the program. Once the Dough cycle is complete, remove the dough from the bread machine. On a floured surface, knead the dough briefly, then roll out to your desired pizza size.
4. Topped with your favorite ingredients, and baked in a preheated oven at 425°F (220°C) for 15-20 minutes, depending on the toppings and desired crust crispiness or until the cheese is bubbly and golden brown.

Nutritional per Serving: 200 calories, 6g protein, 37g carbohydrates, 4g fat, 2g fiber, 0mg cholesterol, 290mg sodium, 50mg potassium.

Tip: Refrigerate dough overnight after Dough cycle, then warm to room temperature for 1 hour before shaping for best flavor and texture.

C. Focaccia Bread Recipes

117. *Classic Herb Focaccia Bread*

Prep time: 15 minutes | Cook time: 1 hour 20 minutes (Dough cycle + Baking)

1 ½ Pounds Loaf (≈ 12 slices):

- 1 cup + 2 tablespoons lukewarm water
- 3 tablespoons olive oil, plus more for drizzling
- 3 cups bread flour
- 1 ½ teaspoons salt and 2 teaspoons sugar
- 1 ½ teaspoons active dry yeast
- 1 tablespoon dried Italian herbs (rosemary, thyme, oregano)
- Coarse sea salt for sprinkling

2 Pounds Loaf (≈ 16 slices):

- 1 ⅓ cups lukewarm water
- ¼ cup olive oil, plus more for drizzling
- 4 cups bread flour
- 2 teaspoons salt and 2 ½ teaspoons sugar
- 2 teaspoons active dry yeast
- 1 ⅓ tablespoons dried Italian herbs (rosemary, thyme, oregano)
- Coarse sea salt for sprinkling

Directions:

1. In the bread machine pan, add water, olive oil, bread flour, salt, sugar, and yeast as per manufacturer's instructions, then sprinkle dried Italian herbs over flour.
2. Select the Dough cycle on your bread machine and start the program.
3. Once the Dough cycle completes, remove the dough, press it into an oiled baking sheet forming dimples with your fingers. Let it rest for 20-30 minutes, or until slightly puffed.
4. Drizzle additional olive oil over the top and sprinkle with coarse sea salt. Bake in a preheated oven at 400°F for 20-25 minutes, or until golden brown.
5. Let cool on a wire rack before slicing.

Nutritional per Serving: 180 calories, 5g protein, 33g carbohydrates, 4g fat, 1g fiber, 0mg cholesterol, 290mg sodium, 60mg potassium.

Tip: For added flavor and texture, sprinkle chopped fresh rosemary or garlic on top of the bread before baking.

118. *Tomato and Basil Focaccia Bread*

Prep time: 20 minutes | Cook time: 2 hours 20 minutes (Dough cycle + Baking)

1 ½ Pounds Loaf (≈ 12 slices):

- 1 cup + 2 tablespoons lukewarm water
- 2 tablespoons olive oil, plus extra for drizzling
- 3 cups bread flour
- 1 ½ teaspoons salt and 2 teaspoons sugar
- 1 ½ teaspoons active dry yeast
- ½ cup cherry tomatoes, halved
- 2 tablespoons fresh basil leaves, chopped
- Coarse sea salt, for sprinkling

2 Pounds Loaf (≈ 16 slices):

- 1 ⅓ cups lukewarm water
- 3 tablespoons olive oil, plus extra for drizzling
- 4 cups bread flour
- 2 teaspoons salt and 2 ½ teaspoons sugar
- 2 teaspoons active dry yeast
- ⅔ cup cherry tomatoes, halved
- 3 tablespoons fresh basil leaves, chopped
- Coarse sea salt, for sprinkling

Directions:

1. Add lukewarm water and olive oil to the bread machine pan, cover with bread flour, then sprinkle salt, sugar, and yeast evenly on top.
2. Select the Dough cycle on your bread machine and start the program.
3. Once the Dough cycle completes, remove the dough, press it into an oiled baking sheet forming dimples with your fingers. Let it rest for 20-30 minutes, or until slightly puffed.
4. Preheat your oven to 400°F . Press the halved cherry tomatoes and chopped basil leaves into the surface of the dough. Drizzle with additional olive oil and sprinkle with coarse sea salt. Bake for 20 to 25 minutes, or until golden brown and the tomatoes are slightly roasted.
5. Let cool on a wire rack before slicing.

Nutritional per Serving: 190 calories, 5g protein, 31g carbohydrates, 4g fat, 2g fiber, 0mg cholesterol, 300mg sodium, 50mg potassium.

Tip: For a deeper flavor, roast the cherry tomatoes before adding them to the dough.

119. Onion & Cheese Focaccia Bread

Prep time: 20 minutes | Cook time: 2 hours 20 minutes (Dough cycle + Baking)

1 ½ Pounds Loaf (≈ 12 slices):

- 1 cup + 2 tablespoons lukewarm water
- 2 tablespoons olive oil, plus extra for topping
- 3 cups bread flour
- 1 ½ teaspoons salt and 2 teaspoons sugar
- 1 ½ teaspoons active dry yeast
- 1 medium onion, thinly sliced
- ½ cup shredded mozzarella cheese
- 1 tablespoon dried rosemary
- Coarse sea salt, for sprinkling

2 Pounds Loaf (≈ 16 slices):

- 1 ⅓ cups lukewarm water
- 3 tablespoons olive oil, plus extra for topping
- 4 cups bread flour
- 2 teaspoons salt and 2 ½ teaspoons sugar
- 2 teaspoons active dry yeast
- 1 large onion, thinly sliced
- ⅔ cup shredded mozzarella cheese
- 1 ⅓ tablespoons dried rosemary
- Coarse sea salt, for sprinkling

Directions:

1. In the bread machine pan, mix water and olive oil, then add bread flour, salt, and sugar. Create a well in the flour for the yeast.
2. Select the Dough cycle on your bread machine and start the program.
3. Once the Dough cycle is complete, transfer the dough to a lightly oiled baking sheet, stretching it to fit. Let it rest for about 30 minutes.
4. Preheat the oven to 400°F. Distribute the thinly sliced onion and shredded mozzarella cheese evenly over the top of the dough. Sprinkle with dried rosemary and coarse sea salt. Drizzle with additional olive oil. Bake for 20 to 25 minutes, or until golden brown and the cheese is bubbly.
5. Let cool on a wire rack before slicing.

Nutritional per Serving: 200 calories, 6g protein, 32g carbohydrates, 5g fat, 2g fiber, 10mg cholesterol, 350mg sodium, 60mg potassium.

Tip: For a softer texture and deeper flavor, caramelize the onions lightly before topping the focaccia.

120. Olive Focaccia Bread

Prep time: 20 minutes | Cook time: 2 hours 20 minutes (Dough cycle + Baking)

1 ½ Pounds Loaf (≈ 12 slices):

- 1 cup + 2 tablespoons lukewarm water
- 2 tablespoons olive oil, plus extra for drizzling
- 3 cups bread flour
- 1 ½ teaspoons salt and 2 teaspoons sugar
- 1 ½ teaspoons active dry yeast
- ½ cup Kalamata olives, pitted and halved
- 1 tablespoon dried rosemary

2 Pounds Loaf (≈ 16 slices):

- 1 ⅓ cups lukewarm water
- 3 tablespoons olive oil, plus extra for drizzling
- 4 cups bread flour
- 2 teaspoons salt and 2 ½ teaspoons sugar
- 2 teaspoons active dry yeast
- ⅔ cup Kalamata olives, pitted and halved
- 1 ⅓ tablespoons dried rosemary

Directions:

1. Place the lukewarm water and olive oil into the bread machine pan. Add the bread flour, ensuring it covers the liquid. Sprinkle the salt, sugar, and then evenly distribute the yeast on top.
2. Select the Dough cycle on your bread machine and start. The machine will mix, knead, and rise the dough.
3. Once the Dough cycle is complete, transfer the dough to a lightly oiled baking sheet, stretching it to fit. Press the olive halves and sprinkle the dried rosemary onto the dough. Let it rest for about 30 minutes.
4. Preheat your oven to 400°F. Drizzle additional olive oil over the top and bake for 20 to 25 minutes, or until golden brown.
5. Remove from the oven and cool on a wire rack before slicing.

Nutritional per Serving: 190 calories, 5g protein, 32g carbohydrates, 5g fat, 2g fiber, 0mg cholesterol, 400mg sodium, 50mg potassium.

Tip: For a more intense flavor, let the dough rise slowly in the refrigerator overnight before baking.

Chapter 12: Meat Breads

A. Savory Meat-filled Bread Recipes

121. Sausage and Cheddar Bread

Prep Time: 15 minutes | Cook Time: 3 hours 30 minutes

1 ½ Pounds Loaf (≈ 12 slices):

- 1 cup + 2 tablespoons lukewarm water
- 2 tablespoons olive oil
- 3 cups bread flour
- 1 ½ teaspoons salt and 1 tablespoon sugar
- 1 ½ teaspoons active dry yeast
- ½ pound cooked sausage, crumbled and cooled
- 1 cup sharp cheddar cheese, shredded

2 Pounds Loaf (≈ 16 slices):

- 1 ⅓ cups lukewarm water
- 3 tablespoons olive oil
- 4 cups bread flour
- 2 teaspoons salt and 1 ⅓ tablespoons sugar
- 2 teaspoons active dry yeast
- ⅔ pound cooked sausage, crumbled and cooled
- 1 ⅓ cups sharp cheddar cheese, shredded

Directions:

1. In the bread machine pan, first add the lukewarm water and olive oil. Follow with a layer of bread flour, ensuring it completely covers the liquids. Sprinkle the sugar and salt evenly over the flour. Create a small well in the center of the flour and add the yeast.
2. Select the basic or white Bread cycle, and adjust the crust to your preferred setting.
3. At the add-in beep or just before the final kneading cycle ends (≈ 10 min), evenly distribute the cooked, crumbled sausage and shredded cheddar cheese over the dough.
4. Once done, remove the bread from the machine and let it cool before slicing.

Nutritional per Serving: 200 calories, 8g protein, 27g carbohydrates, 7g fat, 1g fiber, 20mg cholesterol, 400mg sodium, 100mg potassium.

Tip: Cooling the sausage completely after cooking and draining it helps to minimize excess grease, ensuring a perfect texture and flavor balance in the bread.

122. Ham and Swiss Bread

Prep time: 15 minutes | Cook time: 3 hours 30 minutes

1 ½ Pounds Loaf (≈ 12 slices):

- 1 cup + 2 tablespoons lukewarm water
- 2 tablespoons olive oil
- 3 cups bread flour
- 1 ½ teaspoons salt
- 1 tablespoon sugar
- 1 ½ teaspoons active dry yeast
- ½ pound cooked ham, diced
- 1 cup Swiss cheese, shredded

2 Pounds Loaf (≈ 16 slices):

- 1 ⅓ cups lukewarm water
- 3 tablespoons olive oil
- 4 cups bread flour
- 2 teaspoons salt
- 1 ⅓ tablespoons sugar
- 2 teaspoons active dry yeast
- ⅔ pound cooked ham, diced
- 1 ⅓ cups Swiss cheese, shredded

Directions:

1. In the bread machine pan, start by adding the lukewarm water and olive oil. Next, add the bread flour, covering the liquid entirely. Evenly sprinkle the salt and sugar over the flour. Make a small well in the center and add the yeast.
2. Select the basic or white Bread cycle, and adjust the crust to your preferred setting.
3. At the add-in beep or just before the final kneading cycle ends (≈ 10 min), pause the machine to add the diced ham and shredded Swiss cheese. Distribute them evenly over the dough.
4. Once done, remove the bread from the machine and let it cool before slicing.

Nutritional per Serving: 220 calories, 10g protein, 27g carbohydrates, 8g fat, 1g fiber, 25mg cholesterol, 450mg sodium, 100mg potassium.

Tip: To ensure the bread has a balanced distribution of ham and cheese, consider giving the ingredients a quick stir after adding them to the dough during the kneading cycle.

123. Salami and Provolone Bread

Prep time: 15 minutes | Cook time: 3 hours 30 minutes

1 ½ Pounds Loaf (≈ 12 slices):

- 1 cup + 2 tablespoons of lukewarm water
- 2 tablespoons of olive oil
- 3 cups of bread flour
- 1 ½ teaspoons of salt and 1 tablespoon of sugar
- 1 ½ teaspoons of active dry yeast
- ½ pound of salami, thinly sliced
- 1 cup of provolone cheese, shredded

2 Pounds Loaf (≈ 16 slices):

- 1 ⅓ cups lukewarm water
- 1 ⅓ cups of lukewarm water
- 3 tablespoons of olive oil
- 4 cups of bread flour
- 2 teaspoons of salt
- 1 ⅓ tablespoons of sugar
- 2 teaspoons of active dry yeast
- ⅔ pound of salami, thinly sliced
- 1 ⅓ cups of provolone cheese, shredded

Directions:

1. In the bread machine pan, start by adding the lukewarm water and olive oil. Next, add the bread flour to fully cover the liquids. Sprinkle the sugar and salt evenly over the flour. Make a small indentation in the center of the flour and carefully place the yeast into it.
2. Select the basic or white Bread cycle, and adjust the crust to your preferred setting.
3. At the add-in beep or just before the final kneading cycle ends (≈ 10 min), pause the machine to evenly distribute the salami slices and shredded provolone cheese over the dough.
4. Allow the bread machine to finish its cycle, including the baking phase. Once done, remove the bread from the machine and let it cool before slicing.

Nutritional per Serving: 200 calories, 9g protein, 27g carbohydrates, 8g fat, 1g fiber, 20mg cholesterol, 500mg sodium, 100mg potassium.

Tip: For optimal flavor, choose high-quality salami and provolone cheese. The better the ingredients, the more delicious your bread will be.

124. Bacon and Onion Bread

Prep time: 25 minutes | Cook time: 3 hours 45 minutes

1 ½ Pounds Loaf (≈ 12 slices):

- 1 cup + 2 tablespoons of lukewarm water
- 2 tablespoons of olive oil
- 3 cups of bread flour
- 1 ½ teaspoons of salt and 1 tablespoon of sugar
- 1 ½ teaspoons of active dry yeast
- ½ pound of bacon, cooked, drained, and crumbled
- ½ cup of caramelized onions

2 Pounds Loaf (≈ 16 slices):

- 1 ⅓ cups of lukewarm water
- 3 tablespoons of olive oil
- 4 cups of bread flour
- 2 teaspoons of salt and 1⅓ tablespoons of sugar
- 2 teaspoons of active dry yeast
- ⅔ pound of bacon, cooked, drained, and crumbled
- ⅔ cup of caramelized onions

Directions:

1. Cook the bacon until crisp, then drain and crumble it. Caramelize the onions until they are golden brown and soft. Let both the bacon and onions cool to room temperature.
2. In the bread machine pan, add water and olive oil first. Add bread flour to completely cover the liquids. Evenly sprinkle the salt and sugar over the flour. Make a small indentation in the center of the flour and add the yeast.
3. Select the basic or white Bread cycle, and adjust the crust to your preferred setting.
4. At the add-in beep or just before the final kneading cycle ends (≈ 10 min), evenly distribute the crumbled bacon and caramelized onions over the dough.
5. Once done, remove the bread from the machine and let it cool before slicing.

Nutritional per Serving: 210 calories, 8g protein, 28g carbohydrates, 9g fat, 1g fiber, 15mg cholesterol, 500mg sodium, 100mg potassium.

Tip: Cool bacon and onions before adding to dough to avoid greasy texture and ensure even flavor distribution.

B. Stuffed or Rolled Meat Bread Recipes

125. Chicken and Broccoli Rolled Bread

Prep time: 30 minutes | Cook time: 3 hours 30 minutes

1 ½ Pounds Loaf (≈ 12 slices):

- 1 cup + 2 tablespoons of lukewarm water
- 2 tablespoons of olive oil
- 3 cups of bread flour
- 1 ½ teaspoons of salt and 1 tablespoon of sugar
- 1 ½ teaspoons of active dry yeast
- 1 cup of cooked chicken, shredded
- 1 cup of broccoli, steamed and finely chopped
- 1 cup of cheddar cheese, shredded

2 Pounds Loaf (≈ 16 slices):

- 1 ⅓ cups of lukewarm water
- 3 tablespoons of olive oil
- 4 cups of bread flour
- 2 teaspoons of salt and 1 ⅓ tablespoons of sugar
- 2 teaspoons of active dry yeast
- 1 ⅓ cups of cooked chicken, shredded
- 1⅓ cups of broccoli, steamed and finely chopped
- 1 ⅓ cups of cheddar cheese, shredded

Directions:

1. Place water, olive oil, bread flour, salt, sugar, yeast in the bread machine pan according to the manufacturer's instructions for a dough cycle.
2. Start the dough cycle. While the dough is being prepared, mix the shredded chicken, chopped broccoli, and shredded cheese in a bowl.
3. Once the dough cycle completes, remove the dough and roll it out on a floured surface into a rectangle shape.
4. Spread the chicken, broccoli, and cheese mixture over the dough, then roll it up tightly.
5. Place the roll seam side down in the bread machine pan and set it to the bake-only cycle, or follow your machine's instructions for baking rolled or filled bread, or in an oven at 350°F for 25-30 minutes until golden.

Nutritional per Serving: 220 calories, 10g protein, 30g carbohydrates, 7g fat, 2g fiber, 30mg cholesterol, 400mg sodium, 150mg potassium.

Tip: Let the chicken and broccoli cool completely before adding them to the dough to prevent excess moisture.

126. Buffalo Blue Chicken Rolled Bread

Prep time: 35 minutes | Cook time: 3 hours 35 minutes

1 ½ Pounds Loaf (≈ 12 slices):

- cup + 2 tablespoons of lukewarm water
- 2 tablespoons olive oil
- 3 cups bread flour
- 1 ½ teaspoons salt and 1 tablespoon sugar
- 1 ½ teaspoons active dry yeast
- 1 cup cooked chicken, shredded and mixed with 2 tablespoons buffalo sauce
- ½ cup blue cheese, crumbled
- ¼ cup celery, finely diced

2 Pounds Loaf (≈ 16 slices):

- 1 ⅓ cups of lukewarm water
- 3 tablespoons olive oil
- 4 cups bread flour
- 2 teaspoons salt and 1 ⅓ tablespoons sugar
- 2 teaspoons active dry yeast
- 1 ⅓ cups cooked chicken, shredded and mixed with 3 tablespoons buffalo sauce
- ⅔ cup blue cheese, crumbled
- ⅓ cup celery, finely diced

Directions:

1. Add water and olive oil to the bread machine pan. Cover with bread flour, sprinkle sugar and salt evenly, then make a well for the yeast.
2. Choose the dough cycle to mix, knead, and rise the dough. Then combine the shredded buffalo chicken, crumbled blue cheese, and finely diced celery in a bowl.
3. Once the dough cycle completes, roll out the dough on a floured surface into a rectangle. Spread the buffalo chicken mixture over the dough, then roll it up tightly from the long side.
4. Place the roll seam side down in the machine on bake-only cycle or follow your machine's instructions for baking rolled or filled bread, or in an oven at 350°F for 25 minutes until golden.

Nutritional per Serving: 230 calories, 11g protein, 31g carbohydrates, 8g fat, 1g fiber, 25mg cholesterol, 500mg sodium, 100mg potassium.

Tip: Cool buffalo chicken mixture to room temperature before adding to dough to prevent sogginess.

127. Beef and Mushroom Stuffed Bread

Prep time: 35 minutes | Cook time: 3 hours 40 minutes

1 ½ Pounds Loaf (≈ 12 slices):

- 1 cup + 2 tablespoons lukewarm water
- 2 tablespoons olive oil
- 3 cups bread flour
- 1 ½ teaspoons salt and 1 tablespoon sugar
- 1 ½ teaspoons active dry yeast
- 1 cup cooked ground beef, drained
- 1 cup mushrooms, sautéed and cooled
- ½ cup mozzarella cheese, shredded

2 Pounds Loaf (≈ 16 slices):

- 1 ⅓ cups lukewarm water
- 3 tablespoons olive oil
- 4 cups bread flour
- 2 teaspoons salt and 1 ⅓ tablespoons sugar
- 2 teaspoons active dry yeast
- 1 ⅓ cups cooked ground beef, drained
- 1 ⅓ cups mushrooms, sautéed and cooled
- ⅔ cup mozzarella cheese, shredded

Directions:

1. In the bread machine pan, mix water and olive oil. Cover with bread flour, sprinkle salt and sugar evenly, and create a well for the yeast. Add the yeast to the well.
2. Use the dough setting for mixing, kneading, and rising. Then combine the cooked ground beef, cooled sautéed mushrooms, and shredded mozzarella cheese in a bowl.
3. After the dough cycle completes, roll out the dough on a floured surface into a rectangle. Spread beef, mushroom, and cheese on dough, leave a border, roll up, and seal edges.
4. Transfer the rolled dough back into the bread machine pan and select the bake cycle. If your machine does not support custom baking cycles, preheat your oven to 350°F and bake for 25-30 minutes, or until golden brown.

Nutritional per Serving: 240 calories, 12g protein, 32g carbohydrates, 8g fat, 2g fiber, 30mg cholesterol, 400mg sodium, 200mg potassium.

Tip: Drain beef and cool mushrooms before mixing with cheese to prevent excess moisture and ensure perfect bread texture.

128. Pulled Pork Coleslaw Stuffed Bread

Prep time: 45 minutes | Cook time: 3 hours 40 minutes

1 ½ Pounds Loaf (≈ 12 slices):

- 1 cup + 2 tablespoons of lukewarm water
- 2 tablespoons olive oil
- 3 cups bread flour
- 1 ½ teaspoons salt and 1 tablespoon sugar
- 1 ½ teaspoons active dry yeast
- 1 cup pulled pork, precooked
- 1 cup coleslaw (cabbage, carrot mix) drained
- 2 tbsp. barbecue sauce (mix with pulled pork)

2 Pounds Loaf (≈ 16 slices):

- 1 ⅓ cups lukewarm water
- 3 tablespoons olive oil
- 4 cups bread flour
- 2 teaspoons salt and 1 ⅓ tablespoons sugar
- 2 teaspoons active dry yeast
- 1 ⅓ cups precooked pulled pork
- 1⅓ cups drained coleslaw (cabbage, carrot mix)
- 3 tbsp. barbecue sauce (mix with pulled pork)

Directions:

1. In the bread machine pan, mix water and olive oil. Cover with bread flour, sprinkle salt and sugar evenly, and create a well for the yeast. Add the yeast to the well.
2. Use the dough setting for mixing, kneading, and rising. Then combine the pulled pork with barbecue sauce, and ensure the coleslaw mix is well-drained to remove excess moisture.
3. Once the dough cycle is complete, roll out the dough on a floured surface into a rectangle. Spread pulled pork and coleslaw evenly on dough, roll up tightly, and seal ends.
4. Transfer the rolled dough back into the bread machine pan and select the bake cycle. If your machine does not support custom baking cycles, preheat your oven to 350°F and bake for 25-30 minutes, or until golden brown.

Nutritional per Serving: 230 calories, 11g protein, 31g carbohydrates, 8g fat, 1g fiber, 25mg cholesterol, 500mg sodium, 100mg potassium.

Tip: Cool buffalo chicken mixture to room temperature before adding to dough to prevent sogginess.

C. Seasoned Meat Bread Recipes

129. Teriyaki Beef Bread

Prep time: 25 minutes | Cook time: 3 hours 35 minutes

1 ½ Pounds Loaf (≈ 12 slices):

- 1 cup + 2 tablespoons lukewarm water
- 2 tablespoons olive oil
- 3 cups bread flour
- 1 ½ teaspoons salt and 1 tablespoon sugar
- 1 ½ teaspoons active dry yeast
- 1 cup beef, cooked and thinly sliced
- ¼ cup teriyaki sauce (mix with beef)
- 2 tablespoons green onions, finely chopped

2 Pounds Loaf (≈ 16 slices):

- 1 ⅓ cups water, lukewarm
- 3 tablespoons olive oil
- 4 cups bread flour
- 2 teaspoons salt and 1 ⅓ tablespoons sugar
- 2 teaspoons active dry yeast
- 1 ⅓ cups beef, cooked and thinly sliced
- ⅓ cup teriyaki sauce (mix with beef)
- 3 tablespoons green onions, finely chopped

Directions:

1. Add water and olive oil to the bread machine pan. Cover with bread flour, sprinkle sugar and salt evenly, then make a well for the yeast.
2. Choose the dough cycle to mix, knead, and rise the dough. Then mix thinly sliced beef with teriyaki sauce, marinate briefly, then stir in chopped green onions.
3. Once the dough cycle completes, remove the dough, flatten it on a lightly floured surface, and evenly distribute the teriyaki beef mixture over it. Roll the dough carefully to enclose the filling and seal the ends.
4. Place the roll seam side down in the machine on bake-only cycle or follow your machine's instructions for baking rolled or filled bread, or in an oven at 350°F for 25 minutes until golden.

Nutritional per Serving: 230 calories, 10g protein, 36g carbohydrates, 6g fat, 2g fiber, 20mg cholesterol, 500mg sodium, 150mg potassium.

Tip: Marinate teriyaki beef to enhance flavor and cool to room temperature before adding to prevent dough overheating.

130. Garlic and Herb Shrimp Bread

Prep time: 20 minutes | Cook time: 3 hours 25 minutes

1 ½ Pounds Loaf (≈ 12 slices):

- 1 cup + 2 tablespoons lukewarm water
- 2 tablespoons olive oil
- 3 cups bread flour
- 1 ½ teaspoons salt and 1 tablespoon sugar
- 1 ½ teaspoons active dry yeast
- 1 cup shrimp, cooked, peeled, finely chopped
- 1 tbsp. fresh herbs (parsley, dill, etc.), chopped
- 1 garlic clove, minced
- ½ teaspoon black pepper

2 Pounds Loaf (≈ 16 slices):

- 1 ⅓ cups water, lukewarm
- 3 tablespoons olive oil
- 4 cups bread flour
- 2 teaspoons salt and 1 ⅓ tablespoons sugar
- 2 teaspoons active dry yeast
- 1 ⅓ cups shrimp, cooked, peeled, finely chopped
- 1⅓ tbsp. fresh herbs (parsley, dill, etc.), chopped
- 2 garlic cloves, minced
- ⅔ teaspoon black pepper

Directions:

1. Add water and olive oil to the bread machine pan. Cover with bread flour, sprinkle sugar and salt evenly, then make a well for the yeast.
2. Choose the dough cycle to mix, knead, and rise the dough. Then mix shrimp, garlic, herbs, and pepper in a bowl; Ensure mixture is room temperature to preserve yeast activity.
3. After the dough cycle completes, take out the dough, roll it on a lightly floured surface, and spread the shrimp mixture evenly on top. Roll the dough back into a loaf shape, seal the ends.
4. Place the roll seam side down in the machine on bake-only cycle or follow your machine's instructions for baking rolled or filled bread, or in an oven at 350°F for 25 minutes until golden.

Nutritional per Serving: 215 calories, 10g protein, 34g carbohydrates, 4g fat, 2g fiber, 50mg cholesterol, 390mg sodium, 95mg potassium.

Tip: Cool buffalo chicken mixture to room temperature before adding to dough to prevent sogginess.

131. Spiced Tuna Bread

Prep time: 25 minutes | Cook time: 3 hours 40 minutes

1 ½ Pounds Loaf (≈ 12 slices):

- 1 cup + 2 tablespoons lukewarm water
- 2 tablespoons olive oil
- 3 cups bread flour
- 1 ½ teaspoons salt and 1 tablespoon sugar
- 1 ½ teaspoons active dry yeast
- 1 cup canned tuna, drained and flaked
- 1 tsp. dried dill and 1 tsp. paprika
- ½ teaspoon black pepper
- 2 tablespoons red onion, finely chopped

2 Pounds Loaf (≈ 16 slices):

- 1 ⅓ cups lukewarm water
- 3 tablespoons olive oil
- 4 cups bread flour
- 2 teaspoons salt and 1 ⅓ tablespoons sugar
- 2 teaspoons active dry yeast
- 1 ⅓ cups canned tuna, drained and flaked
- 1 ⅓ tsp. dried dill and 1 ⅓ tsp. paprika
- ⅔ teaspoon black pepper
- 3 tablespoons red onion, finely chopped

Directions:

1. Add water and olive oil to the bread machine pan. Cover with bread flour, sprinkle sugar and salt evenly, then make a well for the yeast.
2. Choose the dough cycle to mix, knead, and rise the dough. Then, in a bowl, mix the flaked tuna with dill, paprika, black pepper, and finely chopped red onion.
3. Once the dough cycle completes, remove the dough and flatten it on a lightly floured surface. Evenly spread the tuna mixture over the dough. Roll the dough back into a loaf shape, ensuring the filling is evenly distributed.
4. Place the roll seam side down in the machine on bake-only cycle or follow your machine's instructions for baking rolled or filled bread, or in an oven at 350°F for 25 minutes until golden.

Nutritional per Serving: 210 calories, 11g protein, 34g carbohydrates, 4g fat, 2g fiber, 15mg cholesterol, 450mg sodium, 120mg potassium.

Tip: Drain and flake tuna well to evenly spread flavor without extra moisture.

132. Savory Turkey and Sage Bread

Prep time: 25 minutes | Cook time: 3 hours 45 minutes

1 ½ Pounds Loaf (≈ 12 slices):

- 1 cup + 2 tablespoons lukewarm water
- 2 tablespoons olive oil
- 3 cups bread flour
- 1 ½ teaspoons salt and 1 tablespoon sugar
- 1 ½ teaspoons active dry yeast
- 1 cup cooked turkey, finely chopped
- 2 tablespoons fresh sage, finely chopped
- ½ tsp. garlic powder and ½ tsp. onion powder

2 Pounds Loaf (≈ 16 slices):

- 1 ⅓ cups lukewarm water
- 3 tablespoons olive oil
- 4 cups bread flour
- 2 teaspoons salt and 1 ⅓ tablespoons sugar
- 2 teaspoons active dry yeast
- 1 ⅓ cups cooked turkey, finely chopped
- 3 tablespoons fresh sage, finely chopped
- ½ tsp. garlic powder and ½ tsp. onion powder

Directions:

1. In the bread machine pan, begin by adding the lukewarm water and olive oil. Next, add the bread flour, ensuring it completely covers the liquid. Sprinkle the salt and sugar over the flour, then make a small well in the center and add the yeast.
2. Select the basic or white Bread cycle, and adjust the crust to your preferred setting.
3. At the add-in beep or just before the final kneading cycle ends (≈ 10 min), evenly distribute the finely chopped cooked turkey (cook the turkey in advance), fresh sage, garlic powder, and onion powder over the dough.
4. Select the basic or white Bread cycle, and adjust the crust to your preferred setting.
5. Once done, remove the bread from the machine and let it cool before slicing.

Nutritional per Serving: 210 calories, 9g protein, 34g carbohydrates, 5g fat, 2g fiber, 20mg cholesterol, 390mg sodium, 110mg potassium.

Tip: Ensure the turkey is not too moist to prevent soggy bread. Freshly chopped sage enhances bread flavor, perfect for your meal.

Chapter 13: Sourdough Breads

A. Sourdough White Bread Recipes

133. Sourdough White Bread with Starter

Prep Time: 15 minutes | Cook Time: 3 hours 50 minutes

1 ½ Pounds Loaf (≈ 12 slices):

- ¾ cup sourdough starter, active and fed
- ⅔ cup lukewarm water
- 2 tablespoons olive oil
- 3 cups bread flour
- 1 ½ teaspoons salt
- 1 tablespoon sugar
- 2 teaspoons active dry yeast

2 Pounds Loaf (≈ 16 slices):

- 1 cup sourdough starter, active and fed
- 1 cup lukewarm water
- 2 ½ tablespoons olive oil
- 4 cups bread flour
- 2 teaspoons salt
- 1 ⅓ tablespoons sugar
- 2 ½ teaspoons active dry yeast

Directions:

1. Add the sourdough starter, lukewarm water, and olive oil to the bread machine pan. Next, add the bread flour, covering the liquid entirely. Evenly sprinkle the salt and sugar over the flour. Make a small well in the center and add the yeast.
2. Select sourdough, white or classic bread cycle with longer fermentation if possible. Adjust the crust to your preferred setting.
3. Start the bread-making cycle for mixing, kneading, rising (including longer sourdough fermentation), and baking.
4. Once done, remove the bread from the machine and let it cool before slicing.

Nutritional per Serving: 210 calories, 6g protein, 40g carbohydrates, 3g fat, 2g fiber, 0mg cholesterol, 390mg sodium, 80mg potassium.

Tip: Ensure sourdough starter is active and bubbly. Use the sourdough setting if available for longer fermentation. Remember, the quality of the starter affects bread's flavor and rise.

134. Sourdough White Bread with Beer

Prep time: 25 minutes | Cook time: 3 hours 50 minutes

1 ½ Pounds Loaf (≈ 12 slices):

- ¾ cup sourdough starter, active
- ½ cup beer (lukewarm lager or pale ale)
- ¼ cup lukewarm water
- 2 tablespoons olive oil
- 3 cups bread flour
- 1 ½ teaspoons salt
- 1 tablespoon sugar
- 2 teaspoons active dry yeast

2 Pounds Loaf (≈ 16 slices):

- 1 cup sourdough starter, active
- ⅔ cup beer (lukewarm lager or pale ale)
- ⅓ cup water, lukewarm
- 3 tablespoons olive oil
- 4 cups bread flour
- 2 teaspoons salt
- 1 ⅓ tablespoons sugar
- 2 ½ teaspoons active dry yeast

Directions:

1. In the bread machine pan, mix the sourdough starter, beer, lukewarm water, and olive oil.
2. Layer the bread flour over the wet mixture, ensuring it completely covers the liquids. Sprinkle the salt and sugar around the edges of the flour. Make a small well in the center of the flour (but not down to the liquid) and add the yeast.
3. Select sourdough, white or classic bread cycle with longer fermentation if possible. Adjust the crust to your preferred setting.
4. Start the bread-making cycle for mixing, kneading, rising (including longer sourdough fermentation), and baking.
5. Once done, remove the bread from the machine and let it cool before slicing.

Nutritional per Serving: 200 calories, 6g protein, 37g carbohydrates, 3g fat, 2g fiber, 0mg cholesterol, 300mg sodium, 100mg potassium.

Tip: For a deeper flavor, choose a beer with more robust notes, such as a stout or porter. Ensure the beer is at room temperature to not affect the yeast's activity negatively.

135. Maple Bacon Sourdough White Bread

Prep Time: 20 minutes | Cook Time: 4 hours

1 ½ Pounds Loaf (≈ 12 slices):

- ¾ cup sourdough starter, active
- ½ cup lukewarm water
- 2 tablespoons maple syrup
- 2 tablespoons olive oil
- 3 cups bread flour
- 1 ½ teaspoons salt
- 2 teaspoons active dry yeast
- ½ cup bacon, cooked and crumbled

2 Pounds Loaf (≈ 16 slices):

- 1 cup sourdough starter, active
- ⅔ cup lukewarm water
- 3 tablespoons maple syrup
- 3 tablespoons olive oil
- 4 cups bread flour
- 2 teaspoons salt
- 2 ½ teaspoons active dry yeast
- ⅔ cup bacon, cooked and crumbled

Directions:

1. In the bread machine pan, combine the sourdough starter, lukewarm water, maple syrup, and olive oil. Then, gently add the bread flour over the liquid mixture, ensuring it's evenly spread. Sprinkle the salt around the outer edge of the flour. Make a small well in the center of the flour and carefully add the yeast.
2. Select sourdough, white or classic bread cycle with longer fermentation if possible. Adjust the crust to your preferred setting.
3. At the add-in beep or just before the final kneading cycle ends (≈ 10 min), pause the machine to incorporate the bacon manually.
4. Allow the bread machine to finish its cycle, including the baking phase. If your machine lacks custom cycles for shaped dough, bake in an oven at 375°F for 25 minutes until golden. After baking, cool the bread before slicing.

Nutritional per Serving: 210 calories, 7g protein, 38g carbohydrates, 4g fat, 1g fiber, 10mg cholesterol, 400mg sodium, 90mg potassium.

Tip: Brush bread with maple syrup in the last 10 minutes of baking and use well-drained, crumbled bacon to avoid greasy dough.

136. Chocolate Sourdough White Bread

Prep time: 20 minutes | Cook time: 4 hours

1 ½ Pounds Loaf (≈ 12 slices):

- ¾ cup sourdough starter, active
- ⅔ cup lukewarm water
- 2 tablespoons sugar and 1 ½ teaspoons salt
- 2 tablespoons unsalted butter, melted
- 3 cups bread flour
- 2 teaspoons active dry yeast
- ½ cup semi-sweet chocolate chips

2 Pounds Loaf (≈ 16 slices):

- 1 cup sourdough starter, active
- 1 cup water, lukewarm
- 2 ½ tablespoons sugar and 2 teaspoons salt
- 3 tablespoons unsalted butter, melted
- 4 cups bread flour
- 2 ½ teaspoons active dry yeast
- ¾ cup semi-sweet chocolate chips

Directions:

1. In the bread machine pan, combine the sourdough starter, lukewarm water, sugar, and melted butter. Then add the bread flour, ensuring it fully covers the liquid ingredients. Sprinkle the salt around the flour's perimeter. Make a small indentation in the center of the flour and add the yeast.
2. Select sourdough, white or classic bread cycle with longer fermentation if possible. Adjust the crust to your preferred setting.
3. At the add-in beep or just before the final kneading cycle ends (≈ 7 min), pause the machine to incorporate the chocolate chips manually.
4. Allow the bread machine to finish its cycle, including the baking phase. Select a light crust setting to prevent chocolate burning, if available. After baking, cool the bread before slicing.

Nutritional per Serving: 230 calories, 5g protein, 35g carbohydrates, 7g fat, 2g fiber, 10mg cholesterol, 350mg sodium, 80mg potassium.

Tip: Ensure the sourdough starter is active for proper rise. Add chocolate chips late in the second kneading cycle to keep chunks intact. Ideal for breakfast or sandwiches.

B. Sourdough Multigrain Bread Recipes

137. Basic Sourdough Multigrain Bread

Prep Time: 20 minutes | Cook Time: 4 hours

1 ½ Pounds Loaf (≈ 12 slices):

- 1 cup sourdough starter, at room temperature
- ¾ cup lukewarm water
- 2 tablespoons olive oil
- 2 tablespoons honey
- 1 ½ teaspoons salt
- 1 ½ cups bread flour, 1 ½ cups whole wheat flour
- ½ cup multigrain cereal mix
- 1 ½ teaspoons bread machine yeast

2 Pounds Loaf (≈ 16 slices):

- 1⅓ cups sourdough starter, at room temperature
- 1 cup lukewarm water
- 2 ½ tablespoons olive oil
- 2 ½ tablespoons honey
- 2 teaspoons salt
- 2 cups bread flour, 2 cups whole wheat flour
- ⅔ cup multigrain cereal mix
- 2 teaspoons bread machine yeast

Directions:

1. In the bread machine pan, mix the sourdough starter, lukewarm water, honey and olive oil. Next, add the whole wheat and bread flour, covering the liquid entirely. Evenly sprinkle the salt and multigrain cereal mix over the flour. Make a small well in the center and add the yeast.
2. Select sourdough, white or classic bread cycle with longer fermentation if possible. Adjust the crust to your preferred setting.
3. When the timer beeps, check the dough. If it's too wet, add a tablespoon of flour at a time. If it's too dry, add a teaspoon of water at a time until the desired consistency is reached.
4. Once done, remove the bread from the machine and let it cool before slicing.

Nutritional per Serving: 180 calories, 6g protein, 36g carbohydrates, 3g fat, 4g fiber, 0mg cholesterol, 290mg sodium, 110mg potassium.

Tip: For richer flavor, rest dough after first kneading for 10-12 hours before baking. This unlocks the full potential of the sourdough and grains.

138. Walnut Whole Wheat Sourdough Bread

Prep time: 20 minutes | Cook time: 4 hours

1 ½ Pounds Loaf (≈ 12 slices):

- 1 cup sourdough starter, at room temperature
- ¾ cup lukewarm water
- 1 tablespoon olive oil
- 2 tablespoons honey
- 1 ½ teaspoons salt
- 2 ¼ cups whole wheat flour
- ¼ cup multigrain cereal mix
- ½ cup chopped walnuts
- 1 ½ teaspoons bread machine yeast

2 Pounds Loaf (≈ 16 slices):

- 1⅓ cups sourdough starter, at room temperature
- 1 cup lukewarm water
- 1 ½ tablespoons olive oil
- 2 ½ tablespoons honey
- 2 teaspoons salt
- 3 cups whole wheat flour
- ⅓ cup multigrain cereal mix
- ⅔ cup chopped walnuts
- 2 teaspoons bread machine yeast

Directions:

1. In the bread machine pan, mix the sourdough starter, lukewarm water, honey and olive oil. Next, add the whole wheat flour, covering the liquid entirely. Evenly sprinkle the salt and chopped walnuts over the flour. Make a small well in the center and add the yeast
2. Select sourdough, white or classic bread cycle with longer fermentation if possible. Adjust the crust to your preferred setting.
3. When the timer beeps, check the dough. If it's too wet, add a tablespoon of flour at a time. If it's too dry, add a teaspoon of water at a time until the desired consistency is reached.
4. Once done, remove the bread from the machine and let it cool before slicing.

Nutritional per Serving: 220 calories, 8g protein, 44g carbohydrates, 3g fat, 6g fiber, 0mg cholesterol, 290mg sodium, 160mg potassium.

Tip: For optimal sourdough rise, use the starter at peak activity. Cool room temperature optimizes whole wheat's protein, ensuring a digestible carb structure and a successful, natural ferment.

139. Seeded Sourdough Multigrain Bread

Prep Time: 20 minutes | Cook Time: 4 hours

1 ½ Pounds Loaf (≈ 12 slices):

- 1 cup sourdough starter, at room temperature
- ¾ cup lukewarm water
- 1 tablespoon olive oil
- 2 tablespoons honey
- 1 ½ teaspoons salt
- 1 ½ cups bread flour, ¾ cup whole wheat flour
- ½ cup multigrain cereal mix
- ¼ cup mixed seeds (sunflower, pumpkin, flaxseed, sesame seeds)
- 1 ½ teaspoons bread machine yeast

2 Pounds Loaf (≈ 16 slices):

- 1⅓ cup sourdough starter, at room temperature
- 1 cup lukewarm water
- 2 tablespoon olive oil
- 3 tablespoons honey
- 2 teaspoons salt
- 2 cups bread flour, 1 cup whole wheat flour
- ⅔ cup multigrain cereal mix
- ⅓ cup mixed seeds (sunflower, pumpkin, flaxseed, seeds)
- 2 teaspoons bread machine yeast

Directions:

1. In the bread machine pan, mix the sourdough starter, lukewarm water, olive oil and honey. Add the whole wheat and bread flour, covering the liquid entirely. Evenly sprinkle the salt and multigrain cereal mix over the flour. Make a small well in the center and add the yeast.
2. Select sourdough, white or classic bread cycle with longer fermentation if possible. Adjust the crust to your preferred setting.
3. At the add-in beep or just before the final kneading cycle ends (≈ 10 min), pause the machine to add the mixed seeds manually.
4. Once done, remove the bread from the machine and let it cool before slicing.

Nutritional per Serving: 190 calories, 6g protein, 35g carbohydrates, 4g fat, 3g fiber, 0mg cholesterol, 300mg sodium, 140mg potassium.

Tip: For a nuttier flavor and extra crunch, lightly toast the sunflower seeds before adding them to the bread dough.

140. Banana Sourdough Multigrain Bread

Prep time: 20 minutes | Cook time: 4 hours

1 ½ Pounds Loaf (≈ 12 slices):

- ¾ cup sourdough starter, at room temperature
- ½ cup mashed ripe banana (1 medium banana)
- ½ cup lukewarm water
- 1 tablespoon olive oil
- 3 tablespoons honey
- 1 ½ teaspoons salt
- 1 ½ cups bread flour, 1 cup whole wheat flour
- ½ cup multigrain cereal mix
- 1 ½ teaspoons bread machine yeast

2 Pounds Loaf (≈ 16 slices):

- 1 cup sourdough starter, at room temperature
- ⅔ cup mashed ripe banana (1 large banana)
- ⅔ cup lukewarm water
- 2 tablespoons olive oil
- ¼ cup honey
- 2 teaspoons salt
- 2 cups bread flour, 1 ⅓ cups whole wheat flour
- ⅔ cup multigrain cereal mix
- 2 teaspoons bread machine yeast

Directions:

5. In the bread machine pan, mix the sourdough starter, lukewarm water, olive oil and mashed banana. Add the whole wheat and bread flour, covering the liquid entirely. Evenly sprinkle the salt over the flour. Make a small well in the center and add the yeast.
6. Select sourdough, white or classic bread cycle with longer fermentation if possible. Adjust the crust to your preferred setting.
7. Check the dough after 5 minutes of mixing. It should form a soft, tacky ball. If it's too wet, add a tablespoon of flour at a time. If it's too dry, add a teaspoon of water at a time until the desired consistency is reached.
8. Once done, remove the bread from the machine and let it cool before slicing.

Nutritional per Serving: 180 calories, 5g protein, 35g carbohydrates, 2g fat, 4g fiber, 0mg cholesterol, 300mg sodium, 150mg potassium.

Tip: For an extra hint of sweetness and moisture in your bread, consider adding an additional tablespoon of mashed banana to the recipe.

C. Herb Sourdough Bread Recipes

141. Dill and Garlic Sourdough Bread

Prep Time: 15 minutes | Cook Time: 4 hours

1 ½ Pounds Loaf (≈ 12 slices):

- 1 cup sourdough starter, at room temperature
- ¾ cup lukewarm water
- 2 tablespoons olive oil
- 1 tablespoon honey
- 1 ½ teaspoons salt
- 3 cups bread flour
- 1 tablespoon dried dill weed
- 2 garlic cloves, minced
- 1 ½ teaspoons bread machine yeast

2 Pounds Loaf (≈ 16 slices):

- 1 ⅓ cups sourdough starter, at room temperature
- 1 cup lukewarm water
- 2 ½ tablespoons olive oil
- 1 ½ tablespoons honey
- 2 teaspoons salt
- 4 cups bread flour
- 1 ½ tablespoons dried dill weed
- 3 garlic cloves, minced
- 2 teaspoons bread machine yeast

Directions:

1. In the bread machine pan, mix the sourdough starter, lukewarm water, honey and olive oil. Add the bread flour on top, then sprinkle the dried dill weed and minced garlic evenly over the flour. Make a small well in the center and add the yeast.
2. Select sourdough, white or classic bread cycle with longer fermentation if possible. Adjust the crust to your preferred setting.
3. Check the dough during the kneading cycle. If it's too wet, add a tablespoon of flour at a time. If it's too dry, add a teaspoon of water at a time until the desired consistency is reached.
4. Once done, remove the bread from the machine and let it cool before slicing.

Nutritional per Serving: 190 calories, 6g protein, 37g carbohydrates, 2.5g fat, 1g fiber, 0mg cholesterol, 320mg sodium, 80mg potassium.

Tip: For a more intense garlic flavor, roast the garlic cloves before mincing and adding them to the dough.

142. Cilantro Lime Sourdough Bread

Prep time: 20 minutes | Cook time: 4 hours

1 ½ Pounds Loaf (≈ 12 slices):

- 1 cup sourdough starter, at room temperature
- ¾ cup lukewarm water
- Juice of 1 lime (about 2 tablespoons)
- Zest of 1 lime
- 2 tablespoons olive oil
- 1 tablespoon sugar and 1 ½ teaspoons salt
- 3 cups bread flour
- ¼ cup chopped fresh cilantro
- 1 ½ teaspoons bread machine yeast

2 Pounds Loaf (≈ 16 slices):

- 1 ⅓ cups sourdough starter, at room temperature
- 1 cup lukewarm water
- Juice of 1 ½ limes (about 3 tablespoons)
- Zest of 1 ½ limes
- 2 ½ tablespoons olive oil
- 1 ½ tablespoons sugar and 2 teaspoons salt
- 4 cups bread flour
- ⅓ cup chopped fresh cilantro
- 2 teaspoons bread machine yeast

Directions:

1. Add the sourdough starter, lukewarm water, lime juice, lime zest, olive oil, and sugar to the bread machine pan. Then, add the salt and bread flour. Sprinkle the chopped cilantro over the flour. Make a small well in the center of the flour and add the yeast.
2. Select sourdough, white or classic bread cycle with longer fermentation if possible. Adjust the crust to your preferred setting.
3. During the kneading cycle, check the dough. It should be slightly tacky but not overly sticky. If necessary, adjust by adding a little more flour or water, a teaspoon at a time, until the desired consistency is achieved.
4. Once done, remove the bread from the machine and let it cool before slicing.

Nutritional per Serving: 180 calories, 5g protein, 35g carbohydrates, 2.5g fat, 1g fiber, 0mg cholesterol, 320mg sodium, 50mg potassium.

Tip: Boost cilantro-lime flavor by adding an extra tablespoon of chopped cilantro and a teaspoon of lime zest before the final knead.

143. Oregano and Feta Sourdough Bread

Prep Time: 20 minutes | Cook Time: 4 hours

1 ½ Pounds Loaf (≈ 12 slices):

- 1 cup sourdough starter, at room temperature
- ¾ cup lukewarm water
- 2 tablespoons olive oil
- 1 tablespoon honey
- 1 ½ teaspoons salt
- 3 cups bread flour
- 2 teaspoons dried oregano
- ½ cup crumbled feta cheese
- 1 ½ teaspoons bread machine yeast

2 Pounds Loaf (≈ 16 slices):

- 1 ⅓ cups sourdough starter, at room temperature
- 1 cup lukewarm water
- 2 ½ tablespoons olive oil
- 1 ½ tablespoons honey
- 2 teaspoons salt
- 4 cups bread flour
- 1 tablespoon dried oregano
- ⅔ cup crumbled feta cheese
- 2 teaspoons bread machine yeast

Directions:

1. In the bread machine pan, combine the sourdough starter, lukewarm water, olive oil, and honey. Then, add the salt and bread flour on top. Sprinkle the dried oregano over the flour, and then distribute the crumbled feta cheese evenly. Create a well in the flour mix and add yeast.
2. Select sourdough, white or classic bread cycle with longer fermentation if possible. Adjust the crust to your preferred setting.
3. Check dough consistency during the first knead cycle. If it's too dry, add a teaspoon of water at a time. If too wet, add a tablespoon of flour at a time until the right consistency is achieved.
4. Once done, remove the bread from the machine and let it cool before slicing.

Nutritional per Serving: 200 calories, 6g protein, 35g carbohydrates, 4g fat, 1g fiber, 10mg cholesterol, 400mg sodium, 50mg potassium.

Tip: For an extra burst of flavor, consider adding a tablespoon of chopped fresh oregano to the dough along with the feta for a fresher, more vibrant oregano taste.

144. Chive and Parmesan Sourdough Bread

Prep time: 20 minutes | Cook time: 4 hours

1 ½ Pounds Loaf (≈ 12 slices):

- 1 cup sourdough starter, at room temperature
- ¾ cup lukewarm water
- 2 tablespoons olive oil
- 1 tablespoon sugar
- 1 ½ teaspoons salt
- 3 cups bread flour
- ¼ cup freshly grated Parmesan cheese
- 3 tablespoons finely chopped fresh chives
- 1 ½ teaspoons bread machine yeast

2 Pounds Loaf (≈ 16 slices):

- 1 ⅓ cups sourdough starter, at room temperature
- 1 cup lukewarm water
- 2 ½ tablespoons olive oil
- 1 ½ tablespoons sugar
- 2 teaspoons salt
- 4 cups bread flour
- ⅓ cup freshly grated Parmesan cheese
- ¼ cup finely chopped fresh chives
- 2 teaspoons bread machine yeast

Directions:

1. Place the sourdough starter, lukewarm water, olive oil, and sugar into the bread machine pan. Then, add the salt and bread flour. Sprinkle the freshly grated Parmesan cheese and finely chopped chives over the flour. Create a well in the flour mix and add yeast.
2. Select sourdough, white or classic bread cycle with longer fermentation if possible. Adjust the crust to your preferred setting.
3. Check dough consistency during the first knead cycle. If it's too dry, add a teaspoon of water at a time. If too wet, add a tablespoon of flour at a time until the right consistency is achieved.
4. Once done, remove the bread from the machine and let it cool before slicing.

Nutritional per Serving: 190 calories, 6g protein, 36g carbohydrates, 3g fat, 1g fiber, 5mg cholesterol, 330mg sodium, 60mg potassium.

Tip: For an extra layer of flavor and a crispy crust, brush the top of the dough with olive oil and sprinkle a small amount of Parmesan cheese and chopped chives on it before the final rise.

Chapter 14: Seasonal Breads

A.Christmas Bread Recipes

145. Stollen

Stollen, a traditional German fruit bread, is rich with history dating back to the 15th century. Originating from Dresden, it is famously enjoyed during Christmas time. This festive loaf is laden with dried fruits, nuts, spices, and often marzipan, then dusted with powdered sugar, symbolizing the infant Jesus in swaddling clothes.

Prep Time: 30 minutes (plus soaking time for fruits) | Cook Time: 3 hours 30 minutes

1 ½ Pounds Loaf (≈ 12 slices):

- ¼ cup raisins
- ¼ cup dried currants
- ¼ cup chopped candied citrus peel
- 2 tablespoons rum or orange juice
- ¾ cup milk, lukewarm
- 3 cups bread flour
- ¼ cup sugar and ½ teaspoon salt
- 1 ½ teaspoons yeast
- 1 teaspoon ground cinnamon
- ¼ teaspoon ground nutmeg
- ¼ cup unsalted butter, melted
- 1 egg, beaten
- ¼ cup slivered almonds
- ¼ cup chopped marzipan or almond paste
- Powdered sugar for dusting

2 Pounds Loaf (≈ 16 slices):

- ⅓ cup raisins and ⅓ cup dried currants
- ⅓ cup chopped candied citrus peel
- 3 tablespoons rum or orange juice
- 1 cup milk, lukewarm
- 4 cups bread flour
- ⅓ cup sugar and ¾ teaspoon salt
- 2 teaspoons yeast
- 1 ¼ teaspoons ground cinnamon
- ⅓ teaspoon ground nutmeg
- ⅓ cup unsalted butter, melted
- 1 large egg, beaten
- ⅓ cup slivered almonds
- ⅓ cup chopped marzipan or almond paste
- Powdered sugar for dusting

Directions:

1. Soak the raisins, currants, and candied citrus peel in rum or orange juice for at least 2 hours, preferably overnight, to enhance their flavor and plumpness.
2. Place the milk, soaked fruits (including any liquid), melted butter, beaten egg, sugar, and then the flour in your bread machine pan. Sprinkle the salt, cinnamon, and nutmeg around the edges of the flour. Make a small indentation in the center of the flour and add the yeast.
3. Select the Dough setting on your bread machine and start the cycle. After the initial mixing and before the first rise, gently incorporate the slivered almonds and chopped marzipan into the dough by hand or using a dough hook.
4. Once the dough cycle is complete, remove the dough, shape it into a traditional stollen loaf (a folded oval), and allow it to rise in a warm place for about 1 hour or until doubled in size.
5. Bake in a preheated oven at 350°F (175°C) for 25-30 minutes for the 1 ½ pound loaf or 35-40 minutes for the 2-pound loaf, or until the bread is golden brown and sounds hollow when tapped on the bottom. Cool on a wire rack and dust with powdered sugar before serving.

Nutritional per Serving: 250 calories, 6g protein, 45g carbohydrates, 5g fat, 2g fiber, 25mg cholesterol, 150mg sodium, 100mg potassium.

Tip: For an even more flavorful Stollen, it's highly recommended to let the dried fruits—raisins, mixed candied fruits, and chopped almonds—soak in rum overnight, rather than just an hour. This extended marination not only softens the fruits, making them juicier and more delightful to bite into, but also deeply infuses the bread with a luxurious, rich taste that's reminiscent of traditional holiday celebrations. The rum not only adds a depth of flavor but also complements the spices like cinnamon and nutmeg, enhancing the overall aroma and taste of the Stollen. This small step can transform your bread from good to unforgettable, making it a highlight of your festive table.

146. Panettone

Panettone, an iconic Italian Christmas bread, hails from Milan and boasts a centuries-old legacy. Characterized by its dome shape, the bread is a culinary masterpiece that combines candied fruits, raisins, and a distinctive light, airy texture achieved through a lengthy fermentation process. Traditionally, it symbolizes luck and prosperity, making it a staple of festive celebrations. Its popularity has transcended Italian borders, making it a beloved holiday treat worldwide.

Prep time: 30 minutes | Cook time: 3 hours 50 minutes

1 ½ Pounds Loaf (≈ 12 slices):

- ½ cup mixed candied fruit
- ¼ cup raisins
- 3 tablespoons rum or orange juice
- ⅔ cup milk, lukewarm
- 2 ¾ cups bread flour
- ¼ cup sugar
- 1 ½ teaspoons yeast
- ½ teaspoon salt
- 2 eggs, beaten
- 4 tablespoons unsalted butter, softened
- 1 teaspoon vanilla extract
- Zest of 1 orange
- Zest of 1 lemon
- ¼ cup sliced almonds (for topping)

2 Pounds Loaf (≈ 16 slices):

- ⅔ cup mixed candied fruit
- ⅓ cup raisins
- ¼ cup rum or orange juice
- ¾ cup milk, lukewarm
- 3 ⅔ cups bread flour
- ⅓ cup sugar
- 2 teaspoons yeast
- ¾ teaspoon salt
- 3 eggs, beaten
- 5 tablespoons unsalted butter, softened
- 1 ¼ teaspoons vanilla extract
- Zest of 1 ½ oranges
- Zest of 1 ½ lemons
- ⅓ cup sliced almonds (for topping)

Directions:

1. Soak the mixed candied fruit and raisins in rum or orange juice for at least 2 hours, or overnight, to plump them up.
2. Add the milk, soaked fruits (with any leftover liquid), sugar, beaten eggs, softened butter, vanilla extract, and the zest of orange and lemon into the bread machine pan. Then add the bread flour on top, spreading it out to cover the wet ingredients. Sprinkle the salt around the outside and make a small well in the center of the flour for the yeast.
3. Select the Dough setting on your bread machine. Once the dough cycle is complete, if the machine has a baking option, you can let it continue, or remove the dough, shape it into a round loaf, and place it in a panettone mold or a high-sided cake pan.
4. Cover and let rise in a warm place until doubled in size, about 1 hour. Then, bake in a preheated oven at 350°F (175°C) for about 40-45 minutes for the 1 ½ pound loaf or 50-55 minutes for the 2-pound loaf, or until golden and a skewer inserted into the center comes out clean.
5. Once baked, cool on a wire rack and sprinkle the top with sliced almonds. Serve dusted with powdered sugar if desired.

Nutritional per Serving: 220 calories, 5g protein, 38g carbohydrates, 5g fat, 2g fiber, 55mg cholesterol, 150mg sodium, 100mg potassium.

Tip: To capture the essence of an authentic Italian Panettone, consider allowing the bread to cool upside down after it's finished baking. This method, often employed in traditional Italian bakeries, involves suspending the Panettone by skewers through its bottom, then inverting it to cool. This not only prevents the delicate, airy structure from collapsing under its own weight during the cooling process but also ensures the crumb remains light and fluffy, embodying the hallmark texture of this classic holiday treat. Furthermore, this technique enhances the distribution of fruits within the bread, ensuring every slice is evenly rich in flavor and texture. Adopting this cooling method can transform your homemade Panettone into a masterpiece that rivals those found in the finest Italian pâtisseries, making it a luxurious addition to your festive celebrations.

147. Pulla (Finnish Cardamom Bread)

Prep time: 30 minutes | Cook time: 3 hours 30 minutes

1 ½ Pounds Loaf (≈ 12 slices):

- 1 cup lukewarm milk
- 3 ¼ cups bread flour
- ¼ cup sugar and ½ teaspoon salt
- 1 ½ teaspoons yeast
- 1 teaspoon ground cardamom
- 2 tablespoons unsalted butter, melted
- 1 egg, beaten (reserve a little for egg wash)
- ¼ cup raisins
- Pearl sugar or sliced almonds for topping

2 Pounds Loaf (≈ 16 slices):

- 1 ⅓ cups lukewarm milk
- 4 ⅓ cups bread flour
- ⅓ cup sugar and ¾ teaspoon salt
- 2 teaspoons yeast
- 1 ¼ teaspoons ground cardamom
- 3 tablespoons unsalted butter, melted
- 2 eggs, beaten (reserve a little for egg wash)
- ⅓ cup raisins
- Pearl sugar or sliced almonds for topping

Directions:

1. In the bread machine pan, mix milk, melted butter, sugar, beaten eggs raisins, then cover with bread flour. Sprinkle salt and cardamom on the edges, create a well in the center, and add yeast.
2. Choose Dough setting on the machine. Once done, remove dough, divide on a floured surface, and braid or shape as desired. Then Place shaped dough on a parchment-lined baking sheet, cover, and let rise in a warm place until nearly doubled, about 45 minutes to 1 hour.
3. Preheat the oven to 350°F. Brush the risen dough with the reserved beaten egg and sprinkle with pearl sugar or sliced almonds.
4. Bake for ≈30 minutes or until golden brown and the bread sounds hollow when tapped on the bottom. Let it cool on a wire rack before slicing.

Nutritional per Serving: 220 calories, 6g protein, 40g carbohydrates, 4g fat, 2g fiber, 30mg cholesterol, 150mg sodium, 90mg potassium.

Tip: Cover cooling Pulla with a towel to trap steam and soften the crust.

148. Condensed Milk (Innovative Japanese Bread)

Prep time: 15 minutes | Cook time: 3 hours

1 ½ Pounds Loaf (≈ 12 slices):

- ½ cup condensed milk
- ½ cup water, lukewarm
- 2 tablespoons unsalted butter, melted
- 1 teaspoon salt
- 3 cups bread flour
- 2 teaspoons active dry yeast

2 Pounds Loaf (≈ 16 slices):

- ⅔ cup condensed milk
- ⅔ cup water, lukewarm
- 2 ½ tablespoons unsalted butter, melted
- 1 ¼ teaspoons salt
- 4 cups bread flour
- 2 ½ teaspoons active dry yeast

Directions:

1. In the bread machine pan, combine the lukewarm water and condensed milk, stirring gently to mix. Add the melted butter and salt.
2. Add the bread flour, covering the liquid ingredients completely. Make a small indentation on top of the flour (but not so deep it reaches the liquid) and add the yeast into this indentation.
3. Set your bread machine to the Basic or White Bread setting, and choose a light crust color if your machine has crust color options. Start the bread machine.
4. Once the baking cycle is complete, carefully remove the bread pan from the machine using oven mitts, turn out the bread onto a wire rack, and allow it to cool completely before slicing. This ensures the bread slices neatly and has the best texture.

Nutritional per Serving: 190 calories, 5g protein, 35g carbohydrates, 3g fat, 1g fiber, 10mg cholesterol, 200mg sodium, 80mg potassium.

Tip: For a richer flavor and softer crust, brush the top of the bread with a little extra melted butter immediately after it comes out of the bread machine. This adds a subtle buttery flavor and keeps the crust soft.

B. Easter Bread Recipes

149. Italian Easter Bread

Italian Easter Bread, a symbol of rebirth and resurrection, is a sweet, yeasted bread often baked into a wreath shape to represent the crown of thorns. Traditionally, it incorporates colorful hard-boiled eggs, symbolizing new life, nestled within its braided dough. The bread is richly flavored with citrus zest and anise, offering a light, airy texture. This festive bread is a staple during Easter celebrations in Italy, embodying the joy and renewal of spring.

Prep Time: 20 minutes | Cook Time: 3 hours 30 minutes

1 ½ Pounds Loaf (≈ 12 slices):

- ½ cup milk, lukewarm
- 3 cups bread flour
- ¼ cup sugar
- 2 teaspoons active dry yeast
- ½ teaspoon salt
- ¼ cup unsalted butter, melted
- 2 eggs, lightly beaten
- 1 teaspoon vanilla extract
- ½ teaspoon lemon zest
- ½ teaspoon orange zest
- ¼ cup mixed candied fruit
- ¼ cup raisins
- 1 lightly beaten egg (for egg wash)
- Colored sprinkles (for decoration)

2 Pounds Loaf (≈ 16 slices):

- ⅔ cup milk, lukewarm
- 4 cups bread flour
- ⅓ cup sugar
- 2 ½ teaspoons active dry yeast
- ¾ teaspoon salt
- ⅓ cup unsalted butter, melted
- 3 eggs, lightly beaten
- 1 ¼ teaspoons vanilla extract
- ¾ teaspoon lemon zest
- ¾ teaspoon orange zest
- ⅓ cup mixed candied fruit
- ⅓ cup raisins
- 1 lightly beaten egg (for egg wash)
- Colored sprinkles (for decoration)

Directions:

1. Add the lukewarm milk, beaten eggs (reserving a bit for the egg wash), melted butter, sugar, and salt to the bread machine pan. Next, add the bread flour, covering the wet ingredients completely. Make a well in the center of the flour and add the yeast.
2. Set the bread machine to the Dough setting. After the dough cycle completes, remove the dough and divide it into three equal parts. Roll each part into a long rope, about 18 inches long for the 1 ½ pounds loaf or 24 inches for the 2 pounds loaf.
3. Braid the three ropes together gently and place the braid in a greased bread pan or on a baking sheet lined with parchment paper, forming a circle or a traditional braid shape.
4. Cover the braided dough with a clean towel and let it rise in a warm place until nearly doubled in size, about 1 hour.
5. Preheat your oven to 350°F (175°C). Brush the top of the risen braid with the reserved beaten egg. Bake for 25-30 minutes for the 1 ½ pounds loaf or 30-35 minutes for the 2 pounds loaf, until golden brown.
6. Mix the powdered sugar, milk, and vanilla extract to make the glaze. Drizzle the glaze over the warm bread and sprinkle with colored sprinkles for a festive appearance.

Nutritional per Serving: 250 calories, 7g protein, 42g carbohydrates, 5g fat, 1g fiber, 60mg cholesterol, 150mg sodium, 90mg potassium.

Tip: To elevate your Italian Easter Bread to a show-stopping centerpiece, consider giving it a luxurious, glossy finish by applying an egg wash right before baking. This simple yet effective technique involves beating an egg with a tablespoon of water and gently brushing the mixture over the surface of your shaped dough. Not only does this provide a stunning golden sheen to the crust, making it visually appealing and festive, but it also adds a subtle richness to the flavor profile. Additionally, for a touch of extra elegance and texture, sprinkle the loaf with pearl sugar or sliced almonds after the egg wash. This not only enhances the bread's appearance but also introduces a delightful crunch, contrasting beautifully with the soft, tender crumb inside. This enhanced presentation technique will not only captivate your guests' eyes but also their taste buds, making your Italian Easter Bread the highlight of your Easter celebration.

150.Glazed Braided Easter Bread

Glazed Braided Easter Bread, a visually stunning festive treat, intertwines rich cultural traditions with culinary artistry. This sweet, yeasted bread, often woven into intricate braids, symbolizes unity and strength. Before baking, it's adorned with colorful sprinkles or nestled with dyed Easter eggs, reflecting renewal and life. After baking, a glossy glaze adds a touch of sweetness and elegance, making it a centerpiece at Easter celebrations. Its preparation and sharing embody the spirit of community and rebirth.

Prep Time: 20 minutes | Cook Time: 3 hours 30 minutes

1 ½ Pounds Loaf (≈ 12 slices):

- ¾ cup milk, lukewarm
- 2 large eggs, beaten (reserve a small amount for glaze)
- ¼ cup unsalted butter, melted
- ¼ cup sugar
- ½ teaspoon salt
- 3 ½ cups bread flour
- 2 teaspoons active dry yeast

For the glaze:
- ½ cup powdered sugar
- 2 tablespoons milk
- ½ teaspoon vanilla extract
- Colored sprinkles for decoration

2 Pounds Loaf (≈ 16 slices):

- 1 cup milk, lukewarm
- 3 large eggs, beaten (reserve a small amount for glaze)
- ⅓ cup unsalted butter, melted
- ⅓ cup sugar
- ¾ teaspoon salt
- 4 ½ cups bread flour
- 2 ½ teaspoons active dry yeast

For the glaze:
- ⅔ cup powdered sugar
- 3 tablespoons milk
- ¾ teaspoon vanilla extract
- Colored sprinkles for decoration

Directions:

1. Add the lukewarm milk, melted butter, sugar, beaten eggs (reserving a bit for the egg wash), and salt to the bread machine pan. Next, add the bread flour, covering the wet ingredients completely. Make a well in the center of the flour and add the yeast.
2. Set the bread machine to the Dough setting. After the dough cycle completes, remove the dough and divide it into three equal parts. Roll each part into a long rope, about 18 inches long for the 1 ½ pounds loaf or 24 inches for the 2 pounds loaf.
3. Braid the three ropes together gently and place the braid in a greased bread pan or on a baking sheet lined with parchment paper, forming a circle or a traditional braid shape.
4. Cover the braided dough with a clean towel and let it rise in a warm place until nearly doubled in size, about 1 hour.
5. Preheat your oven to 350°F (175°C). Brush the top of the risen braid with the reserved beaten egg. Bake for 25-30 minutes for the 1 ½ pound loaf or 30-35 minutes for the 2 pounds loaf, until golden brown.
6. Mix the powdered sugar, milk, and vanilla extract to make the glaze. Drizzle the glaze over the warm bread and sprinkle with colored sprinkles for a festive appearance.

Nutritional per Serving: 250 calories, 7g protein, 42g carbohydrates, 5g fat, 1g fiber, 60mg cholesterol, 150mg sodium, 90mg potassium.

Tip: To elevate your Glazed Braided Easter Bread into a truly festive and visually stunning treat, consider adding a sprinkle of colored sugar crystals or nonpareils onto the freshly applied glaze. This simple yet effective embellishment not only introduces a vibrant burst of color, making the bread an eye-catching centerpiece for your Easter table, but also adds a delightful textural contrast with a subtle crunch against the soft, tender bread. Furthermore, to make this Easter bread uniquely yours, you can personalize the glaze with natural food colorings or flavorings such as lemon or almond extract, offering a hint of extra flavor that complements the sweetness of the glaze. This approach transforms a simple braided bread into a bespoke creation that reflects the joy and renewal that Easter symbolizes, making it not just a dish, but a part of the celebration itself.

151. Paska Ukrainian Easter Bread

Prep time: 30 minutes | Cook time: 3 hours 30 minutes

1 ½ Pounds Loaf (≈ 12 slices):

- ½ cup lukewarm milk
- 2 large eggs, beaten
- ¼ cup unsalted butter, melted
- ¼ cup sugar and ½ teaspoon salt
- 3 ¼ cups bread flour
- 2 teaspoons active dry yeast
- ¼ cup raisins (optional)
- 1 teaspoon vanilla extract
- Zest of 1 lemon

2 Pounds Loaf (≈ 16 slices):

- ⅔ cup lukewarm milk
- 3 large eggs, beaten
- ⅓ cup unsalted butter, melted
- ⅓ cup sugar
- ¾ teaspoon salt
- 4 ¼ cups bread flour
- 2 ½ teaspoons active dry yeast
- ⅓ cup raisins (optional)
- 1 ¼ teaspoons vanilla extract
- Zest of 1 ½ lemons

Directions:

1. Mix lukewarm milk, eggs, butter, sugar, vanilla, and lemon zest in the bread machine pan. Cover with bread flour, sprinkle salt on edges, make a well for yeast, and add it. Optionally, add raisins.
2. Select basic or white bread cycle. Adjust the crust to your preferred setting.
3. Once done, remove the bread from the machine and let it cool before slicing.
4. For a traditional Paska presentation, you can optionally form the dough into a round shape after the dough cycle is complete and bake it in the oven at 350°F for about 30 minutes or until the bread is golden brown and sounds hollow when tapped.

Nutritional per Serving: 210 calories, 6g protein, 35g carbohydrates, 4g fat, 1g fiber, 55mg cholesterol, 150mg sodium, 80mg potassium.

Tip: Brush Paska with egg wash (1 beaten egg + 1 tablespoon water) before baking for a shiny crust.

152. Sweet Braided Easter Bread

Prep time: 30 minutes | Cook time: 3 hours 30 minutes

1 ½ Pounds Loaf (≈ 12 slices):

- ⅔ cup milk, lukewarm
- ⅓ cup sugar and ½ teaspoon salt
- ¼ cup unsalted butter, melted
- 2 large eggs, beaten
- 3 ½ cups bread flour
- 2 teaspoons active dry yeast
- 1 teaspoon vanilla extract
- Zest of 1 lemon and 2 tablespoons lemon juice
- ½ cup powdered sugar

2 Pounds Loaf (≈ 16 slices):

- 1 cup milk, lukewarm
- ½ cup sugar and ¾ teaspoon salt
- ⅓ cup unsalted butter, melted
- 3 large eggs, beaten
- 4 ⅔ cups bread flour
- 2 ½ teaspoons active dry yeast
- 1 ¼ teaspoons vanilla extract
- Zest of 1 ½ lemons and 3 tablespoons lemon juice
- ⅔ cup powdered sugar
- 3 tablespoons lemon juice

Directions:

1. In the bread machine pan, mix lukewarm milk, melted butter, sugar, eggs, vanilla, and lemon zest. Cover with bread flour, sprinkle salt around, make a well for yeast, and add it.
2. Select Dough setting. After, divide dough into three, roll into ropes (18-22 inches).
3. Braid the three ropes together gently and place the braid on a baking sheet lined with parchment paper, forming a traditional braid shape. Then Braid ropes and place on a parchment-lined baking sheet and cover with a towel, let rise in a warm place until nearly doubled, about 1 hour.
4. Preheat oven to 350°F. Bake 25-30 minutes until golden. Then combine powdered sugar and lemon juice for glaze; drizzle over warm bread.

Nutritional per Serving: 210 calories, 6g protein, 37g carbohydrates, 4g fat, 1g fiber, 55mg cholesterol, 125mg sodium, 80mg potassium.

Tip: Brush with egg wash and sprinkle sugar on loaf before baking for a shiny, festive crust.

C. Thanksgiving Bread Recipes

153. *Classic Cornbread*

Prep Time: 10 minutes | Cook Time: 1 hours 30 minutes

1 ½ Pounds Loaf (≈ 12 slices):

- 1 cup cornmeal
- 1 cup all-purpose flour
- ¼ cup sugar
- 1 tablespoon baking powder
- ½ teaspoon salt
- 1 cup buttermilk
- ¼ cup unsalted butter, melted
- 2 large eggs

2 Pounds Loaf (≈ 16 slices):

- 1 ⅓ cups cornmeal
- 1 ⅓ cups all-purpose flour
- ⅓ cup sugar
- 1 ⅓ tablespoons baking powder
- ⅔ teaspoon salt
- 1 ⅓ cups buttermilk
- ⅓ cup unsalted butter, melted
- 3 large eggs

Directions:

1. In a large mixing bowl, whisk together the cornmeal, all-purpose flour, sugar, baking powder, and salt. In a separate bowl, mix the buttermilk, melted butter, and eggs until well combined.
2. Add the wet ingredients to the dry ingredients, stirring just until moistened. Do not overmix.
3. If the bread machine has a bake-only function, pour the batter into its pan and bake for 1 hour (1 ½ lbs) or 1 hour 30 minutes (2 lbs). Without this function, preheat the oven to 375°F (190°C), pour batter into a greased pan, and bake for ≈ 25 minutes until a toothpick comes out clean.
4. Allow the cornbread to cool slightly before slicing and serving.

Nutritional per Serving: 180 calories, 5g protein, 28g carbohydrates, 6g fat, 2g fiber, 55mg cholesterol, 300mg sodium, 75mg potassium.

Tip: For a richer taste and extra moist cornbread, add ¼ cup of honey to the batter. It makes cornbread sweeter and softer.

154. *Sweet Potato Bread*

Prep time: 30 minutes | Cook time: 3 hours 30 minutes

1 ½ Pounds Loaf (≈ 12 slices):

- 1 cup mashed sweet potato (cooked, cooled)
- ½ cup water and ¼ cup milk, lukewarm
- 2 tablespoons unsalted butter, melted
- 3 tablespoons brown sugar and ½ teaspoon salt
- 3 cups bread flour
- 1 ½ teaspoons active dry yeast
- ½ teaspoon cinnamon (optional)
- ¼ teaspoon nutmeg (optional)

2 Pounds Loaf (≈ 16 slices):

- 1 ⅓ cups mashed sweet potato (cooked, cooled)
- ⅔ cup water and ⅓ cup milk, lukewarm
- 3 tablespoons unsalted butter, melted
- ¼ cup brown sugar and ¾ teaspoon salt
- 4 cups bread flour
- 2 teaspoons active dry yeast
- ¾ teaspoon cinnamon (optional)
- ⅓ teaspoon nutmeg (optional)

Directions:

1. Mix mashed sweet potato, water, milk, melted butter, brown sugar in the bread machine pan.
2. On top of the wet ingredients, add the bread flour, ensuring it covers everything. Sprinkle the salt, cinnamon, and nutmeg evenly over the flour. Make a small well in the center of the flour and add the yeast to this well.
3. Select basic or whole wheat setting. Adjust the crust to your preferred setting.
4. Start the bread machine. Once done, remove the bread from the machine and let it cool before slicing.
5. Optionally, glaze cooled bread with powdered sugar mixed with milk or orange juice, or enjoy plain.

Nutritional per Serving: 180 calories, 5g protein, 34g carbohydrates, 3g fat, 2g fiber, 10mg cholesterol, 200mg sodium, 80mg potassium.

Tip: For moister bread, use well-cooked, smoothly mashed sweet potatoes to evenly spread moisture and flavor.

155. Buttermilk Drop Biscuits

Prep Time: 10 minutes | Cook Time: 20 minutes

1 ½ Pounds (≈ 12 biscuits):

- 2 ½ cups all-purpose flour
- 1 tablespoon sugar and 1 teaspoon salt
- 2 ½ teaspoons baking powder
- ½ teaspoon baking soda
- ½ cup unsalted butter, cold and cubed
- 1 cup buttermilk, cold
- Extra butter for brushing (optional)

2 Pounds (≈ 16 biscuits):

- 3 ⅓ cups all-purpose flour
- 1 ⅓ tablespoons sugar and 1 ⅓ teaspoons salt
- 3 ⅓ teaspoons baking powder
- ⅔ teaspoon baking soda
- ⅔ cup unsalted butter, cold and cubed
- 1 ⅓ cups buttermilk, cold
- Extra butter for brushing (optional)

Directions:

1. In a large bowl, whisk together the flour, sugar, baking powder, baking soda, and salt. Add the cold, cubed butter and use a pastry blender or your fingertips to work the butter into the flour until the mixture resembles coarse crumbs.
2. Pour in the cold buttermilk and stir just until the dough comes together; do not overmix.
3. Use a spoon or ice cream scoop to drop the dough onto a parchment-lined baking sheet, forming approximately 12 biscuits for the 1 ½ pound recipe or 16 biscuits for the 2 pounds recipe.
4. Bake in a preheated oven at 425°F (220°C) for 15-20 minutes, or until the biscuits are golden brown on top. Optionally, brush the tops with melted butter immediately after removing them from the oven for a richer flavor and softer crust.
5. Allow the biscuits to cool slightly on the baking sheet before serving.

Nutritional per Serving: 200 calories, 4g protein, 25g carbohydrates, 9g fat, 1g fiber, 25mg cholesterol, 400mg sodium, 50mg potassium.

Tip: For fluffier biscuits, ensure your buttermilk and butter are very cold before mixing. This helps create steam pockets during baking for a lighter texture.

156. Classic Southern Biscuits

Prep time: 15 minutes | Cook time: 25 minutes

1 ½ Pounds (≈ 12 biscuits):

- 2 cups all-purpose flour, plus more for dusting
- 1 tablespoon baking powder
- 1 teaspoon sugar
- ½ teaspoon salt
- ¼ teaspoon baking soda
- 6 tablespoons unsalted butter, cold and cubed
- ¾ cup buttermilk, cold

2 Pounds (≈ 16 biscuits):

- 2 ⅔ cups all-purpose flour, plus more for dusting
- 1 ⅓ tablespoons baking powder
- 1 ⅓ teaspoon sugar
- ⅔ teaspoon salt
- ⅓ teaspoon baking soda
- 8 tablespoons unsalted butter, cold and cubed
- 1 cup buttermilk, cold

Directions:

1. In a large mixing bowl, whisk together the flour, baking powder, sugar, salt, and baking soda. Using a pastry blender or your fingers, cut in the cold butter until the mixture resembles coarse crumbs.
2. Gradually add the cold buttermilk to the flour mixture, stirring until a dough forms. Turn the dough out onto a floured surface and knead gently 4 to 5 times.
3. Roll the dough out to about ¾ inch thickness. Using a biscuit cutter or a glass, cut out biscuits and place them on a baking sheet lined with parchment paper.
4. Bake in a preheated oven at 425°F (220°C) for the specified time or until the biscuits are golden brown on top.
5. Remove from the oven and, if desired, brush the tops with melted butter for a richer flavor and a soft crust.

Nutritional per Serving: 180 calories, 4g protein, 24g carbohydrates, 8g fat, 1g fiber, 20mg cholesterol, 300mg sodium, 50mg potassium.

Tip: For flakier biscuits, make sure to use very cold butter and buttermilk. This ensures that the butter melts as the biscuits bake, creating steam pockets that contribute to the flakiness.

Chapter 15: Breads of the World

157. German Rye Bread

Prep time: 20 minutes | Cook time: 3 hours 40 minutes

1 ½ Pounds Loaf (≈ 12 slices):

- 1 cup lukewarm water
- 2 tablespoons molasses
- 1 tablespoon unsalted butter, softened
- 1 ½ cups rye flour and 1 ½ cups bread flour
- 1 teaspoon salt
- 2 teaspoons caraway seeds (optional)
- 2 teaspoons active dry yeast

2 Pounds Loaf (≈ 16 slices):

- 1 ⅓ cups lukewarm water
- 2 ½ tablespoons molasses
- 1 ½ tablespoon unsalted butter, softened
- 2 cups rye flour and 2 cups bread flour
- 1 ⅓ teaspoons salt
- 2 ⅔ teaspoons caraway seeds (optional)
- 2 ⅔ teaspoons active dry yeast

Directions:

1. Mix lukewarm water, molasses, and softened butter in the pan, then evenly layer with rye and bread flour. Sprinkle the salt and caraway seeds (if using) around the edges of the flour. Make a small indentation in the center of the flour and add the yeast.
2. Set your bread machine to the Whole Wheat or Basic cycle, depending on your machine's settings, with a medium crust setting.
3. Start the bread machine. Once done, remove the bread from the machine and let it cool before slicing.
4. For a traditional touch, you can sprinkle some additional caraway seeds on top of the loaf before the final rising phase in the machine.

Nutritional per Serving: 140 calories, 4g protein, 29g carbohydrates, 2g fat, 3g fiber, 5mg cholesterol, 200mg sodium, 100mg potassium.

Tip: For an even richer flavor, consider adding a tablespoon of cocoa powder to the dough mixture. This won't make the bread taste like chocolate but will enhance the rye flavor and give the loaf a deeper color.

158. Mexican Cornbread

Prep time: 10 minutes | Cook time: 3 hours

1 ½ Pounds Loaf (≈ 12 slices):

- 1 cup milk
- ¼ cup unsalted butter, melted
- 1 egg
- 1 ½ cups all-purpose flour and 1 cup cornmeal
- 3 tablespoons sugar and 1 teaspoon salt
- 1 ½ tsp. baking powder and ½ tsp. baking soda
- ½ cup shredded Cheddar cheese
- ½ cup corn kernels (fresh, frozen, or canned)
- 2 tablespoons chopped jalapeños (optional)
- 1 ½ teaspoons dry yeast

2 Pounds Loaf (≈ 16 slices):

- 1 ⅓ cup milk
- ⅓ cup unsalted butter, melted
- 1 large egg
- 2 cups all-purpose flour and 1 ⅓ cup cornmeal
- 1 ⅓ cups sugar and 1 ⅓ teaspoon salt
- 2 tsp. baking powder and ⅔ tsp. baking soda
- ⅔ cup shredded Cheddar cheese
- ⅔ cup corn kernels (fresh, frozen, or canned)
- 2 ⅔ tablespoons chopped jalapeños (optional)
- 2 teaspoons dry yeast

Directions:

1. In a large bowl, mix together the cornmeal, flour, sugar, baking powder, and salt. In a separate bowl, mix together the flour, cornmeal, sugar, baking powder, baking soda, and salt. Add this mixture over the wet ingredients in the bread machine pan.
2. Add the shredded Cheddar cheese, corn kernels, and jalapeños (if using) on top of the flour mixture. Make a small indentation on top of the dry ingredients and add the dry yeast into it.
3. Set the bread machine to the basic bread cycle with a light crust. Start the bread machine.
4. Once done, remove the bread from the machine and let it cool before slicing.

Nutritional per Serving: 210 calories, 6g protein, 30g carbohydrates, 7g fat, 2g fiber, 35mg cholesterol, 430mg sodium, 95mg potassium.

Tip: For a moister cornbread, add an extra tablespoon of butter or milk. Adjust the amount of jalapeños based on your preference for spice.

159. Swedish Rye Crispbread

Prep time: 25 minutes | Cook time: 2 hours 30 minutes

1 ½ Pounds Loaf (≈ 12 slices):

- 1 cup lukewarm water
- 2 tablespoons molasses
- 1 tablespoon unsalted butter, melted
- 1 ½ cups rye flour
- 1 cup whole wheat flour
- ½ teaspoon salt
- 2 teaspoons caraway seeds (optional for traditional flavor)
- 1 ½ teaspoons dry yeast

2 Pounds Loaf (≈ 16 slices):

- 1 ⅓ cups lukewarm water
- 2 ⅔ tablespoons molasses
- 1 ⅓ tablespoons unsalted butter, melted
- 2 cups rye flour
- 1 ⅓ cups whole wheat flour
- ⅔ teaspoon salt
- 2 ⅔ teaspoons caraway seeds (optional for traditional flavor)
- 2 teaspoons dry yeast

Directions:

1. Add the water, molasses, and melted butter to the bread machine pan.
2. In a separate bowl, mix together the rye flour, whole wheat flour, salt, and caraway seeds (if using). Add this mixture to the bread machine pan.
3. Make a small indentation on top of the dry ingredients (but not so deep it reaches the wet layer) and add the dry yeast into it.
4. Set the bread machine to the whole wheat or whole grain setting with a medium crust. Start the bread machine.
5. Once done, remove the bread from the machine and let it cool before slicing.

Nutritional per Serving: 160 calories, 4g protein, 34g carbohydrates, 2g fat, 5g fiber, 0mg cholesterol, 100mg sodium, 150mg potassium.

Tip: For crispier bread, slice thinly and toast before serving. Adjust the amount of caraway seeds according to taste for a more or less pronounced flavor.

160. Greek Olive Bread

Prep time: 10 minutes | Cook time: 3 hours 50 minutes

1 ½ Pounds Loaf (≈ 12 slices):

- 1 cup + 2 tablespoons water (room temperature)
- 2 tablespoons olive oil
- 3 cups bread flour
- 1 ½ teaspoons salt
- 1 tablespoon sugar
- 2 teaspoons dry yeast
- ¾ cup Kalamata olives, pitted and chopped
- 1 teaspoon dried oregano

2 Pounds Loaf (≈ 16 slices):

- 1 ⅓ cups water (room temperature)
- 2 ½ tablespoons olive oil
- 4 cups bread flour
- 2 teaspoons salt
- 1 ⅓ tablespoons sugar
- 2 ½ teaspoons dry yeast
- 1 cup Kalamata olives, pitted and chopped
- 1 ⅓ teaspoons dried oregano

Directions:

1. Place the water and olive oil into the bread machine pan.
2. Add the bread flour to the pan. Then, sprinkle the salt and sugar around the edges of the flour. Make a small indentation on top of the flour and add the dry yeast to the indentation.
3. Sprinkle the chopped olives and dried oregano on top of the flour mixture.
4. Set the bread machine to the basic or white bread setting with a medium crust. Start the bread machine
5. Once done, remove the bread from the machine and let it cool before slicing.

Nutritional per Serving: 180 calories, 5g protein, 32g carbohydrates, 4g fat, 2g fiber, 0mg cholesterol, 400mg sodium, 100mg potassium.

Tip: For a more pronounced olive flavor, lightly press the olives with a fork before adding them to the dough to release their juices.

161. Japanese Milk Bread

Prep time: 20 minutes | Cook time: 3 hours 10 minutes

1 ½ Pounds Loaf (≈ 12 slices):

- 1 cup + 2 tablespoons lukewarm milk
- 2 tablespoons unsalted butter, melted
- 3 cups bread flour
- 2 tablespoons sugar
- 1 teaspoon salt
- 1 tablespoon nonfat dry milk powder
- 1 ½ teaspoons dry yeast

2 Pounds Loaf (≈ 16 slices):

- 1 ⅓ cups lukewarm milk
- 2 ⅔ tablespoons unsalted butter, melted
- 4 cups bread flour
- 2 ⅔ tablespoons sugar
- 1 ⅓ teaspoons salt
- 1 ⅓ tablespoons nonfat dry milk powder
- 2 teaspoons dry yeast

Directions:

1. Add the lukewarm milk and melted butter to the bread machine pan.
2. Over the milk, evenly distribute the bread flour, ensuring it covers the liquid.
3. Add the sugar, salt, and dry milk powder to one corner of the bread pan. Make a small well in the center of the flour (be careful not to go all the way down to the liquid) and add the dry yeast into it.
4. Set your bread machine to the basic or white bread setting with a light crust. Start the bread machine.
5. Once the baking cycle is complete, remove the bread from the pan and let it cool on a wire rack before slicing.

Nutritional per Serving: 220 calories, 6g protein, 40g carbohydrates, 4g fat, 1g fiber, 10mg cholesterol, 200mg sodium, 80mg potassium.

Tip: For a softer crust, brush the top of the bread with melted butter immediately after taking it out of the bread machine.

162. Irish Soda Bread

Prep time: 10 minutes | Cook time: 1 hours 40 minutes

1 ½ Pounds Loaf (≈ 12 slices):

- 1 ¼ cups buttermilk, lukewarm
- 2 tablespoons unsalted butter, softened
- 3 cups all-purpose flour
- 1 ½ teaspoons baking soda
- 1 teaspoon salt
- 3 tablespoons sugar
- ½ cup raisins (optional)

2 Pounds Loaf (≈ 16 slices):

- 1 ⅔ cups buttermilk, lukewarm
- 2 ⅔ tablespoons unsalted butter, softened
- 4 cups all-purpose flour
- 2 teaspoons baking soda
- 1 ⅓ teaspoons salt
- 4 tablespoons sugar
- ⅔ cup raisins (optional)

Directions:

1. Add the lukewarm buttermilk and softened butter to the bread machine pan.
2. In a separate bowl, mix together the all-purpose flour, baking soda, salt, and sugar. Add this mixture over the wet ingredients in the bread machine pan.
3. If using, sprinkle the raisins evenly over the top of the flour mixture.
4. Set the bread machine to the "Quick Bread" or "Cake" setting. Start the bread machine.
5. Once the baking cycle is complete, carefully remove the bread from the pan and let it cool on a wire rack before slicing.

Nutritional per Serving: 180 calories, 4g protein, 36g carbohydrates, 2g fat, 1g fiber, 5mg cholesterol, 400mg sodium, 70mg potassium.

Tip: For a more traditional flavor, add 1 teaspoon of caraway seeds to the dough. Brush the top of the loaf with a little buttermilk before baking for a crispier crust.

163. Turkish Pide Bread

Prep time: 15 minutes | Cook time: 3 hours 10 minutes

1 ½ Pounds Loaf (≈ 12 slices):

- 1 cup + 2 tablespoons warm water (about 110°F)
- 1 tablespoon olive oil
- 3 cups bread flour
- 1 ½ teaspoons sugar
- 1 teaspoon salt
- 1 ½ teaspoons dry yeast
- Sesame seeds or nigella seeds for topping (optional)

2 Pounds Loaf (≈ 16 slices):

- 1 ⅓ cups warm water (about 110°F)
- 1 ⅓ tablespoons olive oil
- 4 cups bread flour
- 2 teaspoons sugar
- 1 ⅓ teaspoons salt
- 2 teaspoons dry yeast
- Sesame seeds or nigella seeds for topping (optional)

Directions:

1. Place the warm water and olive oil into the bread machine pan.
2. Add the bread flour, sugar, and salt to the pan over the liquids. Make a small indentation on top of the flour and add the dry yeast into it.
3. Select the basic or white bread setting on your bread machine with a medium crust option. Start the machine.
4. After the baking cycle is complete, if you prefer, brush the top of the bread with a little water and sprinkle with sesame seeds or nigella seeds, then put it under the broiler for 1-2 minutes to get a crispy, golden top.

Nutritional per Serving: 180 calories, 5g protein, 36g carbohydrates, 2g fat, 2g fiber, 0mg cholesterol, 200mg sodium, 80mg potassium.

Tip: For a more authentic Turkish flavor, mix in 1 teaspoon of ground mahlab (if available) with the flour. This will give the bread a unique taste that's traditional in Turkish pide.

164. Argentinian Pan de Campo

Prep time: 10 minutes | Cook time: 3 hours 10 minutes

1 ½ Pounds Loaf (≈ 12 slices):

- 1 cup + 2 tablespoons lukewarm water
- 2 tablespoons olive oil
- 3 cups all-purpose flour
- 1 ½ teaspoons salt
- 2 tablespoons sugar
- 2 teaspoons dry yeast

2 Pounds Loaf (≈ 16 slices):

- 1 ⅓ cups water, lukewarm
- 2 ⅔ tablespoons olive oil
- 4 cups all-purpose flour
- 2 teaspoons salt
- 2 ⅔ tablespoons sugar
- 2 ½ teaspoons dry yeast

Directions:

1. Place the lukewarm water and olive oil into the bread machine pan.
2. Add the all-purpose flour, ensuring to cover the liquid. Sprinkle the salt and sugar evenly over the flour.
3. Make a small indentation on top of the flour (but not so deep it reaches the liquid) and add the dry yeast into it.
4. Set the bread machine to the basic or white bread setting with a medium crust. Start the bread machine.
5. Once the cycle is complete, remove the bread, let it cool on a wire rack, then slice.

Nutritional per Serving: 180 calories, 4g protein, 36g carbohydrates, 2g fat, 1g fiber, 0mg cholesterol, 290mg sodium, 50mg potassium.

Tip: For a traditional Argentinian flavor, brush the top of the loaf with a little water and sprinkle with coarse sea salt before baking. This adds a delightful crust and enhances the bread's flavor.

165. Brazilian Pão de Queijo

Prep time: 20 minutes | Cook time: 1 hours 30 minutes

1 ½ Pounds Loaf (≈ 12 slices):

- 1 cup milk
- ½ cup water
- ¼ cup unsalted butter
- 2 ½ cups tapioca flour
- 1 teaspoon salt
- 1 ½ cups grated Parmesan cheese
- 2 beaten eggs

2 Pounds Loaf (≈ 16 slices):

- 1 ⅓ cups milk
- ⅔ cup water
- ⅓ cup unsalted butter
- 3 ⅓ cups tapioca flour
- 1 ⅓ teaspoons salt
- 2 cups grated Parmesan cheese
- 2 ⅔ beaten eggs (beat 3 eggs and remove a little)

Directions:

1. Add milk, water, and butter to the bread machine pan. Set the machine to a basic dough setting to warm up the mixture until the butter melts.
2. Pause the machine and add tapioca flour and salt. Restart the dough cycle to mix thoroughly.
3. Slowly incorporate beaten eggs and grated Parmesan cheese until the mixture forms a sticky dough.
4. If your bread machine has a baking cycle for dough, use it; otherwise, preheat your oven to 350°F (175°C), transfer the dough to an oven-proof dish, and bake for about 25-30 minutes or until they are puffed up and golden.
5. Once the cycle is complete, remove the bread, let it cool on a wire rack, then slice.

Nutritional per Serving: 200 calories, 5g protein, 28g carbohydrates, 9g fat, 0g fiber, 55mg cholesterol, 430mg sodium, 30mg potassium.

Tip: For extra cheesy Pão de Queijo, mix in a handful of shredded mozzarella to the dough before the final mixing stage.

166. Indian Naan Bread

Prep time: 20 minutes | Cook time: 15 minutes

1 ½ Pounds Loaf (≈ 12 slices):

- ¾ cup lukewarm water
- 1 teaspoon sugar and 1 teaspoon salt
- 2 tablespoons olive oil and 1 egg
- 2 tablespoons plain yogurt
- 3 cups all-purpose flour
- 1 ½ teaspoons baking powder
- 2 teaspoons dry yeast
- Minced garlic, chopped cilantro for garnish

2 Pounds Loaf (≈ 16 slices):

- 1 cup warm water
- 1 ⅓ teaspoon sugar and 1 ⅓ teaspoon salt
- 2 ⅔ tablespoons olive oil and 1 ⅓ egg
- 2 ⅔ tablespoons plain yogurt
- 4 cups all-purpose flour
- 2 teaspoons baking powder
- 2 ⅔ teaspoons dry yeast
- Minced garlic, chopped cilantro for garnish

Directions:

1. Place the warm water, sugar, olive oil, yogurt, and egg into the bread machine pan. If using, add garlic here for flavored naan.
2. Add the all-purpose flour on top of the wet ingredients. Then sprinkle the salt and baking powder evenly over the flour. Make a small well in the center of the flour and add the dry yeast into it.
3. Set the bread machine to the dough setting and start the machine. Once the dough cycle is complete, take the dough out and divide it into 12(16) equal portions. Roll each portion into a ball, then flatten to form a naan shape.
4. Preheat a skillet or griddle over medium-high heat. Place the naan on the skillet and cook for about 1-2 minutes on each side or until puffed and lightly golden. Brush with butter and sprinkle with cilantro if desired.

Nutritional per Serving: 180 calories, 5g protein, 32g carbohydrates, 3g fat, 1g fiber, 20mg cholesterol, 200mg sodium, 50mg potassium.

Tip: Brush cooked naan with melted butter, sprinkle salt and cilantro. For garlic flavor, add minced garlic to dough.

167. Moroccan Khobz

Prep time: 20 minutes | Cook time: 3 hours 30 minutes

1 ½ Pounds Loaf (≈ 12 slices):

- 1 cup + 2 tablespoons warm water
- 2 tablespoons olive oil
- 3 cups bread flour
- 1 teaspoon salt
- 1 tablespoon sugar
- 2 teaspoons sesame seeds
- 1 ½ teaspoons dry yeast

2 Pounds Loaf (≈ 16 slices):

- 1 ⅓ cups warm water
- 2 ⅔ tablespoons olive oil
- 4 cups bread flour
- 1 ⅓ teaspoon salt
- 1 ⅓ tablespoon sugar
- 2 ⅔ teaspoons sesame seeds
- 2 teaspoons dry yeast

Directions:

1. Add the warm water and olive oil to the bread machine pan.
2. Over the liquid, add the bread flour. Sprinkle the salt and sugar evenly over the flour. Then sprinkle the sesame seeds on top.
3. Make a small indentation in the center of the flour (not too deep to touch the liquid) and add the dry yeast into it.
4. Set the bread machine to the basic or white bread setting with a medium crust. Start the machine.
5. Once the cycle is complete, remove the bread from the machine and let it cool on a wire rack before slicing.

Nutritional per Serving: 190 calories, 5g protein, 35g carbohydrates, 3g fat, 1g fiber, 0mg cholesterol, 200mg sodium, 60mg potassium.

Tip: For a more traditional Moroccan flavor, brush the top of the dough with a mixture of egg yolk and water before baking, and sprinkle additional sesame seeds.

168. Korean Kimchi Bread

Prep time: 15 minutes | Cook time: 3 hours 40 minutes

1 ½ Pounds Loaf (≈ 12 slices):

- 1 cup lukewarm water
- 2 tablespoons sugar and 1 teaspoon salt
- 2 tablespoons vegetable oil
- 3 cups bread flour
- ½ cup well-drained kimchi, chopped
- 2 tablespoons kimchi juice
- 1 tablespoon gochujang (Korean red chili paste)
- 2 teaspoons dry yeast

2 Pounds Loaf (≈ 16 slices):

- 1 ⅓ cups lukewarm water
- 2 ⅔ tablespoons sugar and 1 ⅓ teaspoon salt
- 2 ⅔ tablespoons vegetable oil
- 4 cups bread flour
- ⅔ cup well-drained kimchi, chopped
- 2 ⅔ tablespoons kimchi juice
- 1 ⅓ tablespoon gochujang (Korean red chili paste)
- 2 ⅔ teaspoons dry yeast

Directions:

1. Add the lukewarm water, sugar, and vegetable oil to the bread machine pan.
2. Add the bread flour to the pan, covering the liquid. Sprinkle the salt evenly over the flour.
3. On top of the flour, evenly distribute the chopped kimchi, then drizzle the kimchi juice and gochujang over it. Make a small well in the center of the flour (not too deep) and add the dry yeast.
4. Set the bread machine to the basic or white bread setting with a medium crust. Start the bread machine.
5. Once the baking cycle is complete, remove the bread, let it cool on a wire rack, then slice.

Nutritional per Serving: 190 calories, 5g protein, 36g carbohydrates, 3g fat, 1g fiber, 0mg cholesterol, 400mg sodium, 80mg potassium.

Tip: For a spicier loaf, you can increase the amount of gochujang according to your taste preference.

Chapter 16, Bonus 1:

How to Make Jam in a Bread Machine

169.Strawberry Jam

Prep time: 5 minutes | Cook time: 1 hour

8 oz of Jam:

- 1-pound fresh strawberries, hulled and halved
- ¾ cup granulated sugar
- 1 tablespoon lemon juice

16 oz of Jam:

- 2 pounds fresh strawberries, hulled and halved
- 1 ½ cups granulated sugar
- 2 tablespoons lemon juice

Directions:

1. Place the strawberries in the bread machine pan and crush them lightly with a fork or potato masher. You want some chunks for texture.
2. Add the granulated sugar and lemon juice over the crushed strawberries and stir to combine.
3. Set your bread machine to the jam setting. If your machine does not have a jam setting, use a basic bake setting that allows for stirring and cooking. Start the cycle.
4. Once the cycle is complete, carefully remove the bread pan from the machine. If the jam is too runny, you can run a second jam cycle for a thicker consistency.
5. Pour the hot jam into sterilized jars. Leave to cool at room temperature, then seal and refrigerate. Use within a month for best freshness.

Nutritional per 1 tablespoon: 45 calories, 0g protein, 11g carbohydrates, 0g fat, 0.5g fiber, 0mg cholesterol, 0mg sodium, 15mg potassium.

Tip: For a smoother jam, you can puree the strawberries before adding them to the bread machine. For a variation, mix in a few raspberries or blueberries with the strawberries.

170.Mixed Berry Jam

Prep time: 5 minutes | Cook time: 1 hour

8 oz of Jam:

- 1 cup strawberries, hulled and halved
- ½ cup raspberries
- ½ cup blueberries
- ¾ cup granulated sugar
- 1 tablespoon lemon juice

16 oz of Jam:

- 2 cups strawberries, hulled and halved
- 1 cup raspberries
- 1 cup blueberries
- 1 ½ cups granulated sugar
- 2 tablespoons lemon juice

Directions:

1. Combine the strawberries, raspberries, blueberries, granulated sugar, and lemon juice in the bread machine pan. If desired, lightly mash the berries for a smoother texture.
2. Set your bread machine to the jam setting. If your machine does not have a jam setting, use a basic bake setting that allows for stirring and cooking. Start the cycle.
3. Once the cycle is complete, carefully remove the bread pan using oven mitts. If the jam is too thin for your liking, you can run the jam cycle again or let it thicken as it cools.
4. Pour the hot jam into sterilized jars, leaving a small space at the top. Allow the jam to cool to room temperature before sealing the jars.
5. Store the sealed jars in the refrigerator and use within 4 weeks for best quality.

Nutritional per 1 tablespoon: 50 calories, 0g protein, 13g carbohydrates, 0g fat, 0.5g fiber, 0mg cholesterol, 0mg sodium, 20mg potassium.

Tip: For an extra flavor boost, add a pinch of cinnamon or vanilla extract to the berry mixture before starting the bread machine. This adds a warm, complex flavor to the jam.

171. *Triple Citrus Marmalade*

Prep time: 20 minutes | Cook time: 1 hour 30 minutes

8 oz of Marmalade:

- 1 orange, thinly sliced and seeds removed
- 1 lemon, thinly sliced and seeds removed
- 1 lime, thinly sliced and seeds removed
- 2 cups water
- 1 ½ cups granulated sugar

16 oz of Marmalade:

- 2 oranges, thinly sliced and seeds removed
- 2 lemons, thinly sliced and seeds removed
- 2 limes, thinly sliced and seeds removed
- 4 cups water
- 3 cups granulated sugar

Directions:

1. Combine the thinly sliced orange, lemon, and lime with water in the bread machine pan. If your bread machine has a jam or marmalade setting, use this; otherwise, use a basic bake setting to simmer the mixture.
2. Start the bread machine and let the citrus mixture simmer for about 1 hour. Open the lid carefully and stir occasionally to ensure even cooking.
3. After 1 hour, add the granulated sugar to the mixture and stir well to combine. Continue cooking for another 30 minutes, or until the mixture thickens to a marmalade consistency.
4. Once the cycle is complete, carefully remove the bread pan from the machine. Pour the hot marmalade into sterilized jars, leaving a ¼ inch headspace. Seal the jars while hot.
5. Allow the jars to cool to room temperature, then store in the refrigerator. Use within 4-6 weeks for best quality.

Nutritional per 1 tablespoon: 45 calories, 0g protein, 12g carbohydrates, 0g fat, 0.1g fiber, 0mg cholesterol, 0mg sodium, 10mg potassium.

Tip: For a smoother marmalade, you can blend or mash part of the citrus mixture before adding sugar. Adjust the sugar to taste, especially if you prefer a less sweet or more tart marmalade.

172. *Apple Pear Ginger Jam*

Prep time: 15 minutes | Cook time: 1 hour

8 oz of Jam:

- 1 large apple, peeled, cored, and finely chopped
- 1 large pear, peeled, cored, and finely chopped
- ¼ cup water
- ½ cup granulated sugar
- 1 tablespoon fresh ginger, grated
- 1 tablespoon lemon juice

16 oz of Jam:

- 2 large apples, peeled, cored, and finely chopped
- 2 large pears, peeled, cored, and finely chopped
- ½ cup water
- 1 cup granulated sugar
- 2 tablespoons fresh ginger, grated
- 2 tablespoons lemon juice

Directions:

1. Place the chopped apples, pears, water, and grated ginger into the bread machine pan.
2. Set your bread machine to the jam setting. If your machine does not have a jam setting, use a basic bake setting that allows for stirring and cooking. Start the cycle. As the machine heats and begins to mix the ingredients, slowly add the granulated sugar and lemon juice.
3. Allow the bread machine to complete the jam cycle, which typically lasts about 1 hour. If your machine has a specific setting for jam, ensure it's used; otherwise, use a generic setting that allows for cooking and stirring.
4. Once the cycle is complete, carefully remove the bread pan from the machine. Pour the hot jam into sterilized jars, leaving a ¼ inch headspace.
5. Seal the jars and let them cool to room temperature. Once cooled, store in the refrigerator and use within 4-6 weeks.

Nutritional per 1 tablespoon: 30 calories, 0g protein, 8g carbohydrates, 0g fat, 0.2g fiber, 0mg cholesterol, 0mg sodium, 15mg potassium.

Tip: For a smoother jam, you can blend half of the apple and pear mixture before cooking. Adjust the amount of ginger according to your taste; more ginger will add a spicy kick, while less will give a milder flavor.

173. Summer Fruit Medley Jam

Prep time: 20 minutes | Cook time: 1 hour 10 minutes

8 oz of Jam:

- ½ cup strawberries, hulled and chopped
- ½ cup peaches, peeled and chopped
- ½ cup raspberries
- ½ cup blueberries
- ¾ cup granulated sugar
- 1 tablespoon lemon juice

16 oz of Jam:

- 1 cup strawberries, hulled and chopped
- 1 cup peaches, peeled and chopped
- 1 cup raspberries
- 1 cup blueberries
- 1½ cups granulated sugar
- 2 tablespoons lemon juice

Directions:

1. Combine all the chopped fruit, granulated sugar, and lemon juice in the bread machine pan. If your bread machine has a jam setting, select it; otherwise, select a basic bake setting that allows the mixture to cook and stir.
2. Start the bread machine. Open the lid and stir the mixture a few times during the first 15 minutes to ensure the sugar dissolves completely.
3. Allow the bread machine to complete the cooking cycle, usually around 1 hour. If the jam isn't as thick as you'd like, you can run the cycle again or let it thicken as it cools.
4. Once the cycle is finished, carefully remove the bread pan. Pour the hot jam into sterilized jars, leaving a ¼ inch headspace. Seal the jars and let them cool to room temperature.
5. Store the sealed jars in the refrigerator. Use the jam within 4-6 weeks for the best flavor.

Nutritional per 1 tablespoon: 35 calories, 0g protein, 9g carbohydrates, 0g fat, 0.5g fiber, 0mg cholesterol, 0mg sodium, 20mg potassium.

Tip: For a smoother texture, you can blend or mash part of the fruit before adding it to the bread machine. Adjust the sugar to your taste, especially if your fruit is very ripe and naturally sweet.

174. Mixed Stone Fruit Jam

Prep time: 15 minutes | Cook time: 1 hour 10 minutes

8 oz of Jam:

- ½ cup peaches, peeled and chopped
- ½ cup nectarines, peeled and chopped
- ½ cup plums, peeled and chopped
- ¾ cup granulated sugar
- 1 tablespoon lemon juice

16 oz of Jam:

- 1 cup peaches, peeled and chopped
- 1 cup nectarines, peeled and chopped
- 1 cup plums, peeled and chopped
- 1 ½ cups granulated sugar
- 2 tablespoons lemon juice

Directions:

1. Place the chopped peaches, nectarines, plums, granulated sugar, and lemon juice into the bread machine pan.
2. Select the jam setting on your bread machine. If your machine does not have a jam setting, use a basic bake setting that allows for stirring and cooking.
3. Start the bread machine. Stir the mixture a few times during the first 15 minutes to help dissolve the sugar and ensure an even mix.
4. Allow the bread machine to complete the cycle, usually about 1 hour. If the jam is too thin for your preference, you can run the cycle again or let it thicken as it cools.
5. Once the cycle is finished, carefully remove the bread pan. Pour the hot jam into sterilized jars, leaving a ¼ inch headspace. Seal the jars and let them cool to room temperature.
6. Store the sealed jars in the refrigerator and use within 4-6 weeks for optimal freshness.

Nutritional per 1 tablespoon: 45 calories, 0g protein, 11g carbohydrates, 0g fat, 0.2g fiber, 0mg cholesterol, 0mg sodium, 15mg potassium.

Tip: For a richer flavor, consider adding a small pinch of cinnamon or vanilla extract to the fruit mixture before starting the bread machine. This can add a subtle depth to the jam's taste.

175. Tropical Mixed Fruit Jam

Prep time: 15 minutes | Cook time: 1 hour 10 minutes

8 oz of Jam:

- ¼ cup mango, peeled and finely chopped
- ¼ cup pineapple, finely chopped
- ¼ cup papaya, peeled and finely chopped
- ½ cup granulated sugar
- 1 tablespoon lemon juice

16 oz of Jam:

- ½ cup mango, peeled and finely chopped
- ½ cup pineapple, finely chopped
- ½ cup papaya, peeled and finely chopped
- 1 cup granulated sugar
- 2 tablespoons lemon juice

Directions:

1. Combine the mango, pineapple, papaya, granulated sugar, and lemon juice in the bread machine pan.
2. Set your bread machine to the jam setting. If your machine doesn't have a jam setting, use a basic bake setting that allows for stirring and cooking.
3. Start the bread machine. During the first few minutes, stir the mixture a few times to ensure the sugar dissolves completely.
4. Let the bread machine complete the cycle, typically about 1 hour. Check the consistency of the jam; if it's too thin, you can run the jam cycle again or let it thicken as it cools.
5. Carefully remove the bread pan from the machine once the cycle is complete. Pour the hot jam into sterilized jars, leaving a ¼ inch headspace. Allow the jars to cool to room temperature before sealing.
6. Store the sealed jars in the refrigerator. Use the jam within 4-6 weeks for the best flavor.

Nutritional per 1 tablespoon: 30 calories, 0g protein, 8g carbohydrates, 0g fat, 0.1g fiber, 0mg cholesterol, 0mg sodium, 10mg potassium.

Tip: Adding a bit of grated ginger or a pinch of cinnamon can enhance the tropical flavors of the jam, providing a warm, spicy note that complements the sweetness of the fruits.

176. Autumn Harvest Jam

Prep time: 20 minutes | Cook time: 1 hour

8 oz of Jam:

- ½ cup apples, peeled, cored, and finely chopped
- ½ cup pears, peeled, cored, and finely chopped
- ¼ cup cranberries, fresh or frozen
- ½ cup pumpkin puree
- ¾ cup granulated sugar
- 1 teaspoon cinnamon
- ½ teaspoon nutmeg
- 1 tablespoon lemon juice

16 oz of Jam:

- 1 cup apples, peeled, cored, and finely chopped
- 1 cup pears, peeled, cored, and finely chopped
- ½ cup cranberries, fresh or frozen
- 1 cup pumpkin puree
- 1 ½ cups granulated sugar
- 2 teaspoons cinnamon
- 1 teaspoon nutmeg
- 2 tablespoons lemon juice

Directions:

1. Combine the apples, pears, cranberries, pumpkin puree, granulated sugar, cinnamon, nutmeg, and lemon juice in the bread machine pan.
2. Set your bread machine to the jam setting. If your machine does not have a jam setting, use a basic bake setting that allows for stirring and cooking.
3. Start the bread machine. During the first few minutes, stir the mixture a few times to ensure the sugar dissolves completely.
4. Let the bread machine complete the cycle, typically about 1 hour. Check the consistency of the jam; if it's too thin, you can run the jam cycle again or let it thicken as it cools.
5. Remove the bread pan from the machine once the cycle is complete. Pour the hot jam into sterilized jars, leaving a ¼ inch headspace. Allow the jars to cool to room temperature before sealing.
6. Store the sealed jars in the refrigerator. Use the jam within 4-6 weeks for the best flavor.

Nutritional per 1 tablespoon: 45 calories, 0g protein, 11g carbohydrates, 0g fat, 0.5g fiber, 0mg cholesterol, 0mg sodium, 15mg potassium.

Tip: Add ginger or clove for extra warmth and spice in Autumn Harvest Jam.

Chapter 17, Bonus 2:

Pairing Homemade Breads with Meals

Embarking on a homemade bread-making journey brings not only the joy of baking but also the delight of pairing these aromatic loaves with the perfect meals. Each type of bread, from the simplest white to the most elaborate sourdough, can elevate a meal from good to unforgettable. This chapter aims to guide you through pairing homemade breads from each category with dishes that will complement their flavors, textures, and aromas, turning every meal into a celebration.

Simple White Breads:

- The versatility of simple white breads makes them a perfect companion to almost any meal. Pair a freshly baked, fluffy white loaf with classic chicken noodle soup. The bread's simplicity allows the soup's flavors to shine while providing a comforting texture.

Whole Grain Breads:

- Whole grain breads, with their hearty texture and nutty flavors, pair beautifully with robust dishes. Try serving a slice of whole grain bread alongside a bowl of beef stew or with a hearty lentil salad. Its robustness complements the earthy flavors of legumes and the richness of stews.

Spice, Herb, and Vegetable Breads:

- These aromatic breads are ideal for pairing with simple, creamy dishes. A slice of rosemary bread goes wonderfully with a creamy tomato soup, while a basil and garlic loaf is the perfect side for a classic spaghetti carbonara. The herbs in the bread will highlight the freshness of the dishes.

Breakfast Breads:

- Sweet and savory breakfast breads are a morning delight. Pair a cinnamon raisin bread with a creamy yogurt and fresh fruit for a sweet start or a bacon and cheese bread with scrambled eggs for a hearty breakfast.

Cheese Breads:

- Cheese breads, with their gooey goodness, are perfect for dipping into chili or serving alongside a fresh Caesar salad. The cheese in the bread complements the richness of the chili and the tanginess of the salad dressing.

Fruit Breads:

- Fruit breads offer a sweet note that pairs beautifully with both sweet and savory. A slice of apple bread can be served with pork chops for a harmonious blend of sweet and savory, or try banana bread with a spread of cream cheese for a delightful snack.

Diet Bread:

- Diet breads, lighter and healthier, are wonderful with salads or light vegetable soups. They add a satisfying crunch without overwhelming the delicate flavors of the meal.

Quick Breads:

- Quick breads, easy and versatile, can be paired with both sweet and savory dishes. A zucchini quick bread can accompany a roasted chicken dinner, while a chocolate chip quick bread is a delightful end to a meal, served with coffee or tea.

Focaccia and Pizza Breads:

- These Italian classics are meals in themselves but try pairing focaccia with a balsamic vinegar and olive oil dip as a starter, or serve pizza bread as a side to a classic Caesar salad for an Italian-themed meal.

Meat Breads:

- Meat breads, rich and satisfying, are a meal on their own but can be complemented with a side of roasted vegetables or a simple green salad to add freshness and balance to the meal.

Sourdough Breads:

- The tangy flavor of sourdough bread is perfect for pairing with creamy cheeses, smoked salmon, or as a base for avocado toast. Its robustness also makes it a great companion to hearty soups and stews.

Seasonal Breads:

- Seasonal breads, with ingredients that highlight the time of year, can be paired with meals that celebrate the season. Stollen during the winter holidays pairs beautifully with mulled wine or a spiced tea, creating a festive and cozy atmosphere. Paska, a traditional Easter bread, complements the flavors of a springtime brunch, such as quiches or salads, with its slightly sweet and enriched dough.

Breads of the World:

- Explore global cuisines by pairing these breads with traditional dishes from their country of origin. Serve a slice of Mexican Cornbread with a spicy chili or a savory stew for a meal that warms the heart with its rich flavors and textures.

Jam and Marmalade:

- Homemade jams made in a bread machine are a sweet addition to any bread. Pair your freshly made jams with a variety of breads for breakfast, as a snack, or even as a dessert. The sweetness of the jam will complement both sweet and plain breads, adding a burst of flavor to every bite.

By thoughtfully pairing homemade breads with meals, you can elevate the dining experience, making each meal a memorable one. Experiment with different combinations to discover the perfect pairings that delight your palate.

Wait, Hold on! Excited to claim your exclusive bonuses? Simply scan the QR code found in your cookbook to unlock access to your special treats. Don't miss out on these additional goodies to enhance your culinary journey!

Conclusion

As we reach the conclusion of our journey through the art of bread making, it's important to reflect on the lessons learned, the skills honed, and the joy that comes from creating something as fundamental yet profound as bread. This cookbook has taken you from the basics of understanding your bread machine to exploring a world of breads that spans cultures, ingredients, and techniques. Each chapter was crafted to inspire, educate, and encourage you to delve deeper into the artistry of bread making.

Bread, in its essence, is a simple food, comprising flour, water, salt, and yeast. Yet, the possibilities it presents are endless, transforming these basic ingredients into an array of loaves, each with its unique flavor, texture, and appearance. Through your bread machine, you've learned to harness these possibilities, creating breads that delight the senses and bring comfort to the soul.

The journey began with a brief overview of bread machines, demystifying the process and setting the stage for what would become a comprehensive exploration of bread making. As you embarked on your bread-making journey, you were equipped with the necessary basis to understand the science and art behind each loaf. This foundation was crucial, as it allowed you to appreciate the nuances of bread making, from kneading and rising to baking and storing.

From simple white breads to complex sourdoughs, each chapter offered a new perspective on bread making. You discovered the hearty wholesomeness of whole grain breads, the aromatic allure of spice, herb, and vegetable breads, and the comforting sweetness of breakfast breads. Cheese, fruit, and meat breads introduced you to the concept of bread as a meal in itself, while diet and quick breads showed you how bread making could be adapted to fit any lifestyle or schedule.

The exploration of focaccia, pizza breads, and breads from around the world opened your eyes to the global nature of bread making, revealing how this humble food can bring people together, transcending cultural and geographical boundaries. Seasonal breads reminded you of the rhythms of nature and how they can be celebrated through baking, while the chapter on making jam in a bread machine added a sweet complement to your bread creations.

But beyond the recipes and techniques, this cookbook has been about more than just baking bread. It's been about discovery, creativity, and the joy of sharing. It's a reminder of the simple pleasures in life and the satisfaction that comes from creating something with your own hands.

There will be successes and failures, but each experience is a step towards mastering this ancient craft. The true beauty of bread making lies not just in the final product but in the process itself—the anticipation of the rise, the aroma that fills your kitchen, and the warmth of a freshly baked loaf.

Keep experimenting, keep learning, and most importantly, keep sharing the fruits of your labor with those you love. After all, bread is more than just food; it's a symbol of home, of comfort, and of community.

Thank you for allowing this cookbook to be part of your bread-making journey. May your kitchen always be filled with the warmth of the oven, the scent of fresh bread, and the joy of baking.

Recipes in Alphabetical Order:

Made in the USA
Las Vegas, NV
30 November 2024

12815800R00063